The Official MP3.com Guide to MP3

Michael Robertson

and

Ron Simpson

MP3.com, Inc. • P.O. Box 910091 • San Diego, CA 92121 • www.mp3.com

Library of Congress Catalog Card Number: 99-93134

Production Manager: *Vanessa Moore*
Cover Designer: *Joanna Ebenstein*
Editor: *Sybil Sosin*
Marketing Managers: *Steve Sheiner, Nancy Hammerman*

©1999 MP3.com, Inc.
P.O. Box 910091
San Diego, CA 92191
619-455-2515 • www.mp3.com

To order bulk quantities of this book, please contact MP3.com at the above address.

Printed in the United States of America

ISBN 0-9670574-0-X

This book is dedicated to music fans everywhere.

— Michael Robertson

*I would like to dedicate this book to Judy and Jack
Vorfeld (my Mom and Stepdad). Thanks for everything!
Your love and support through the lean times has given
me the chance to pursue the nontraditional careers of
music and writing for which I am eternally grateful.*

— Ron Simpson

Contents

Introduction

What is MP3? That is the question we hear all the time, and there just isn't a simple answer. It is certainly more than an open file format that makes it possible to convert large audio files into much smaller near-CD-quality MP3 files. MP3 is about freedom. MP3 is about revolution. MP3 is about choice. But for our purposes, it is mostly about music. For us, it has always been about the music. The MP3 revolution is making music more portable, giving the independent musicians of the world a new forum, royally ticking off the old guard who have run the record industry for the past fifty years, and a whole lot more. By the time you read this book, there will probably be another ten or more MP3 books in production and maybe even a few in release. However, most of these books, if not all of them, will completely miss the mark. More than likely, they will focus only on the technology, and that's really only part of the story. MP3ers have a sense of community, as well as an underlying culture that has less to do with the actual technology and more to do with the freedom of musical expression. One of our constitutional rights is the freedom of expression. Musicians exercise that right often in music, but now there is the opportunity to distribute musical ideas to anyone willing to take the time to download an MP3 file. MP3ers are dramatically changing the way the record industry does business, and each and every one of you reading this book is helping to make this long overdue change actually happen.

WHAT THIS BOOK IS ABOUT

The main purpose of this book is to bring the latest information about MP3 players, development software, and playback hardware together all in one place. The tutorials are comprehensive, yet easy to understand. They also function as an in-depth MP3 product tour for those of you looking for the right combination of software and hardware to meet your wants and needs. If a product is inferior, you probably aren't going to find a tutorial featuring said product in this book.

WHAT TO LOOK FOR

MP3 is largely a Windows 95/98/NT phenomenon, with the Mac OS currently in a distant second place. For that reason, the focus of this book is mostly Windows-based technology with a little bit of Mac on the side.

There will be times and places in the book where you might notice that topics are repeated. This is not an Alzheimer's-related problem, but an assumption that most of you will not read this book in the traditional linear method. Instead, you will probably jump all over the place and use the index more than the table of contents. For this reason, each of the tutorials is self-contained under the assumption that you have not read any other part of the book.

ICONS

As you read through this book, you will notice the following four icons popping up from time to time:

 Note.   Notes are intended to offer you little tidbits of additional information that don't quite fit into the current discourse or tutorial. Notes are also used to point you to useful Web sites.

 Tip.   Information that appears as a tip is intended to provide you with invaluable advice that will save you serious time, serious frustration, or a combination of the two.

 Warning.   If you don't like bad things happening to good people, then you'll heed the information that appears as a warning.

 On the Web.   This icon is used to direct you to the MP3.com Web site. It will direct you to downloads, information, or update pages for this book.

BOOK UPDATES

Because technology is moving forward at about warp 10, here's what we've decided to do to keep you up-to-date on all the changes that are happening with regards to this book and MP3 technology: an update Web site! Go to `www.mp3.com/book/` and look for the update link. We will regularly update each section of the book so that you can always stay current. This Web site within the MP3.com site will also provide an opportunity to continually address the questions that readers of the book will ask.

LEGALITIES

Neither the authors nor MP3.com advocate illegal use or distribution of music, sound, or print material (such as lyrics) over the Internet (or anywhere else). When using the tools for ripping and encoding that are featured in this book, please act responsibly. Chapter 9 covers a few of the basics of copyright law and gives you a few commonsense tips on how to stay out of trouble when dealing with the playback of music and sound. Legislation (the Digital Millennium Copyright Act, for example) is going to put some very sharp teeth into enforcement, and those who choose to ignore it may be in danger of violating the current laws. You really don't want a record company to make an example of you, and we don't want to see that happen either. So watch yourself.

COPY PROTECTION

The concept of copy protection is a great one for record companies and recording artists alike. But for the consumer, it is inconvenient. First of all, by forcing any copy-protection scheme on the general public, the record industry is assuming that consumers are thieves. For the most part, this is just not the case. If you purchase an MP3 file and download it to a Mac, should you be able to play it back from a Windows machine as well? We say yes, but the industry says no. Sure, you could burn a CD and then move that CD to the player in any machine you choose, and the problem is solved. Still, if you're going to go to all that trouble, you might as well just buy the CD, use ripping software, load the MP3 tracks into all of your computers, build the playlist you want, and play the music where and when you choose. The fact that most, if not all, music is available on CD (which also doubles as a high-quality digital master) makes any copy-protection scheme that the music industry is going to come up with a moot point. Any serious MP3 pirate is just going to go out and buy (or borrow) a CD, use ripping software, and post the MP3 files on an anonymous Web site. The people that the record industry is seeking protection from will always find a way around any copy-protection scheme that is going to be developed. As long as the recording industry tries to prevent us from listening to music the way we choose to, everyone looses.

ONE FINAL NOTE

What, no CD-ROM comes with this book? When we were in the early development stages of this book, we decided against including a CD-ROM. There's a good reason for this, and it comes down to just how fast MP3 technology is changing. From our perspective, it seems sort of pointless to ship a CD-ROM with software that will be out of date before you buy the book. Instead, we want you to look at the book update section of the MP3.com Web site (www.mp3.com/book/) as your own personal interactive online CD-ROM. As you're reading this book, go online and point your browser to the update site. There, click on the link that is relevant to the chapter you happen to be reading, and you will then have access to the latest updated information for that chapter, as well as links to the download pages of the featured software. That means you will always have instant access to the latest MP3 software.

Enjoy the book, and thanks for showing up for the revolution!

Acknowledgments

I'd like to thank Ron Simpson for his willingness and commitment to taking on this project. All of us at MP3.com value his insight and skill in articulating our vision.

— Michael Robertson

First, I would like to thank the Godfather of the MP3 movement, Michael Robertson, for buying my last book and liking it enough to bring me on board for this project. Next on the list is the entire staff at Moore Creative Services (including Marley); I owe you big time for this one. Of course, I'd like to thank the staff at MP3.com (past and present) for putting together the most comprehensive MP3 resource on the planet. Last but not least are the software and hardware venders that made the MP3-related products featured in the book. A special thanks goes out to everyone at MusicMatch, Sonique, and Diamond Multimedia. Your assistance was invaluable and is greatly appreciated.

— Ron Simpson

About the Authors

MICHAEL ROBERTSON

President and founder of The Z Company, Michael Robertson started MP3.com, a cutting-edge music site that has become a leader on the Internet. His previous endeavors include the founding of Media Minds, Inc., Filez, and MR Mac Software, as well as innumerable projects within the music industry. BAM magazine named Michael as one of the hundred most influential individuals in the music industry.

RON SIMPSON

In the 1980s, as the world of music and technology collided, Ron Simpson was mercilessly sucked into the vortex of MIDI, Multimedia, and finally the Internet. Since surfacing in the aptly named Digital Desert of Phoenix, Arizona, Ron has written three books on Web audio, euthanized his sequencer to become a jazz piano player, and has been polishing up his chops as a Pro Tools editor. This is book number three in Ron's repertoire of book-writing credits.

I Want My MP3!

One of the biggest advantages MP3 possesses is the fact that it is an international standard. An MP3 file produced with one encoder is usable in hundreds of software players on the market. It will play back on a Mac, Win, Linux, or even a WebTV computer. This ubiquity has helped MP3 garner worldwide approval from all computer camps.

— Michael Robertson

IN THIS CHAPTER

- Winamp

- Sonique

- MusicMatch Jukebox 3.0

- Unreal Player

- Windows Media Player

- FreeAmp

- MacAmp

- SoundApp

There is no better place for us to start then with your computer and a few of the most popular and unique MP3 players that currently exist. This chapter will be a guided tour of the basic functions as well as the unique functions. While MP3 currently seems to be a Windows phenomenon, there is also a Mac-based option out there (MacAmp), and while it was still in beta at this writing, it works well. There are also some streaming audio players that can handle MP3 files as streaming files, and we will take a look at these options later on in this chapter.

Note

For the most part, the content in this chapter is Windows-oriented, although Mac users are encouraged to take a stroll through the entire chapter to get a feel for what's out there.

WINDOWS PLAYERS

As we started checking out all the Windows-based MP3 players available (and under development), it became obvious that it would not be possible to do a detailed rundown on each of them. After consultation, we have come up with four of the most influential and/or interesting MP3 players currently available.

WINAMP

There's a rumor going around that Winamp is the most popular MP3 player on the planet, and this happens to be a rumor we believe. Winamp is a shareware player that is available for a mere $10 (go to www.winamp.com and download it if you haven't already). If you've spent any time at MP3.com's Web site, you might notice there are a lot of MP3 players available and you might be wondering what the difference is between Winamp and all the other players out there. To name a few differences: Winamp is more mature (when we wrote this, it was in version 2.09); it's less buggy; and then there are the two thousand or so skins, plug-ins that dance with the music, audio effects plug-ins, and more. Because the plug-in architecture of Winamp is open, many third-party developers are creating free Winamp plug-ins. Overall, Winamp gives the user a lot of options; and for $10, how can you go wrong?

 Warning

Beware of what you download! With all the free plug-ins, shareware, and freeware out there, it is very easy for a bug-infested free download to terminally mess up your system.

Winamp Tour

The Winamp Player is essentially three components: the Player, the Playlist, and the Equalizer. Starting at the heart of the matter, let's tour the Player.

The Player

There are more controls and options on the Winamp Player than you can shake the proverbial stick at. Most of you will be familiar with some of the controls, but just in case, use Figure 1-1 and Table 1-1 for reference.

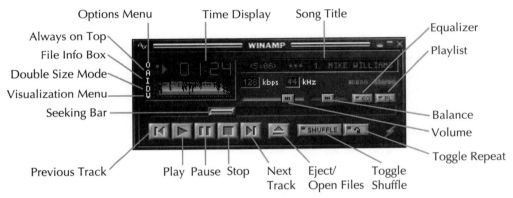

Figure 1-1   The Winamp Player is quick, easy to use, and highly configurable.

The Winamp Playlist

The Winamp Playlist is pretty easy to use. You can drag and drop MP3 files into the Playlist window from the repository folders, and move them in the same fashion. In addition to a miniature set of transport controls (start, stop, and so forth) that duplicates the controls of the Winamp Player, there are five buttons at the bottom of the Playlist window (see Figure 1-2 for reference) that give you access to more functions than you probably want or need. Refer to Figure 1-2 and Table 1-2 for an overview of the different functions that you can access in the Winamp Playlist. The Playlist window is opened and closed by toggling the PL button on the Winamp Player. If you are confused (don't feel bad, it happens) just refer back to Figure 1-1.

Table 1-1   Winamp Player Controls

Function	Description
Options Menu	Access Preferences, Skin Browser, and other options.
Always on Top (Toggle)	This will keep your Winamp Player on top of all applications on your desktop so you can access it immediately, regardless of the application in which you are currently working.
File Info Box	View and edit the track information on an individual MP3 file.
Double Size Mode (Toggle)	Expand the Winamp Player to twice its normal size.
Visualization Menu	Set the look and functions in the visualization meter as well as select, configure, and turn on/off the visual plug-ins.
Previous Track	Return to the previous track in the playlist.
Play	Start playback of a track.
Pause	Pause the track in play.
Next Track	Jump to the next track in the playlist.
Eject/Open Files	If you are listening to an audio CD, this opens the CD player tray; otherwise, it is used to open a file from one of the supported formats.
Seeking Bar	This bar shows you the progress of the song being played. You can drag it to a different location in the current file and playback will resume from that location.
Volume	Adjust the volume.
Balance	Adjust the left/right stereo balance.
Equalizer	Toggle between open/close of the graphic equalizer.
Playlist	Toggle between open/close of the playlist.
Time Display	Displays the elapsed time in the song being played.
Song Title	Displays the artist, song, and length of song.

Note

For more information on how to create and use a Winamp Playlist, refer to Tutorial 2-1, "Creating a Winamp Playlist."

Figure 1-2   The Winamp Playlist window.

 Note

Some of the menu options in Table 1-2 open up additional options. These additional menus are listed in the notes below Table 1-2.

Table 1-2   Winamp Playlist

Function Button	Menu Option 1	Menu Option 2	Menu Option 3	Menu Option 4
+File	Add Files	Add Directory	Add Location (URL)	
-File	Remove Selected	Crop Selected	Clear Playlist	Misc. *
Select All	Select All	Select None	Invert Selection	
Misc. Options	File Info**	Sort***	Misc. ****	
Load List	Open Playlist	Save Playlist	Clear Playlist	

　 *Remove all dead files and physically remove selected file(s).

　 ** File info and playlist entry.

　 *** Sort list by title/sort list by filename/sort list by path and filename/reverse list, and randomize list.

**** Generate HTML playlist and read extended info on section.

More About the Playlist

As you can see from Table 1-2, there are a lot of available options in the Winamp Playlist. You probably load a bunch of files at once and use the old drag-and-drop method to put them in some semblance of order. Toward the latter part of this chapter, we have created a series of Playlist tutorials with regards to Winamp and a few of the other MP3 players that are featured.

The Winamp Equalizer

The Winamp Equalizer is a very straightforward ten-band graphic equalizer (EQ) and preamp. Users can create and save custom EQ and preamp presets, with the icing on the cake being that custom presets can be set to automatically load with a playlist or song. Refer to Figure 1-3 and Table 1-3 for a basic explanation of the Winamp Equalizer functions.

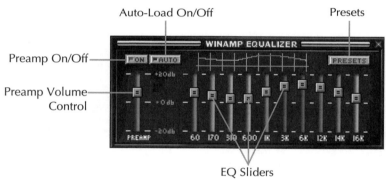

Figure 1-3   The Winamp Equalizer window.

Table1-3   Winamp Equalizer Controls

Function	Description
Preamp (Slider)	This slider boosts or lowers the preamp signal.
Preamp (On/Off Button)	This button turns the Winamp preamp on and off.
Auto	With auto-load engaged, EQ settings previously saved with a song or playlist will load automatically.
Presets	Save, load, or delete an EQ/preamp setting.
EQ Sliders	These ten sliders raise or lower the level of each corresponding frequency. Zero dB (center) is flat.

The Preamp   For those of you unfamiliar with what a preamp is, here's a very simple description: The preamp boosts the audio signal before (as in pre) it arrives at the amplifier. Unless you have really underpowered computer speakers, chances are you will not have to boost the preamp signal too much. Turning the preamp on or off is as simple as clicking the on button in the top left-hand corner of the Winamp Equalizer window.

 Warning

If you boost the preamp signal too much, you will get distortion. Not the warm fuzzy analog distortion that we all love to hear coming from a rock guitar player, but a nasty digital distortion that is more painful to listen to than a Jon Tesh or Barry Manilow concert. You've been warned!

Auto-Load   By enabling the Auto button, any EQ and preamp settings that have been previously saved with a song will be automatically loaded when said song starts playing.

EQ Sliders   Most of you are familiar with the concept of a graphic EQ and how it works. This little overview is for the rest of you. The ten sliders on the Winamp Equalizer are essentially a volume control for each of their assigned frequencies. Zero decibels (0 dB) is considered flat or neutral. Raise or lower a slider, and the frequency assigned to the slider you are moving will be affected. While listening to an MP3 file, experiment a little bit and you'll hear what we're talking about. If you're still a little confused, think of your car (or home) stereo. Most personal stereos have, at the very least, a bass and treble control. Turn up the bass, and the bottom end of what you are listening to gets a boost, or turn up the treble, and whatever you happen to be listening to gets brighter. With a graphic EQ, you are able to fine-tune your listening experience with considerably more distinction. Once more, look directly at the Winamp Equalizer (refer back to Figure 1-3) and the ten sliders. The slider on the far left (60 Hz) is the low bass control, while the slider on the far right (16 kHz) is the high treble control. Everything in between is a graduating variation of bass, midrange, or treble. Again, if you're still not getting this, simply move the sliders while listening, and unless you have serious hearing damage, you will the hear the results.

WHY EQ?

Let's face facts. Most computer users will not even blink at spending $1,500 or more for a computer, but when it comes to computer speakers, they will happily take those free speakers that are part of the package deal when they buy their new CPU. There is a reason they are free — They stink! The point is, when listening to cheap, underpowered speakers, you may have to boost or lower certain frequencies to achieve a more palatable listening experience. This might be because of hearing loss or personal taste (that may differ from that of the artist and producer involved in the recording). Whatever the case, being able to create and save custom EQ (and preamp) presets is a cool option.

Presets   One of the authors has been using the concept of the EQ settings that is found in the Rio Player to create a number of generic presets (rock, jazz, classical) for his Winamp Player. When saving or loading a preset from the Winamp Equalizer, you have four different menu options (refer to Figure 1-5 for reference). If you are new to Winamp or even to the world of Windows-based computers, the following tutorial will show you the basics of saving and loading a Winamp EQ preset.

Tutorial 1-1
SAVING AND LOADING A PRESET

TOOLBOX

- Windows 95/98
- Most current version of Winamp
- Any old MP3 file

On the Web

Go to `www.mp3.com/software/windows/players.html` and click on the link to the Winamp Player if you do not have the latest version of Winamp. Remember that Winamp is shareware. If you haven't already registered, please do so before starting to use it.

1. Launch Winamp and click the EQ button (refer back to Figure 1-1) on the Winamp Player, or use the shortcut **Alt+G** to bring the Winamp Equalizer to the front. Assuming that you have yet to create any EQ presets, your view should look something like that in Figure 1-4, with the Winamp Player and Equalizer staring you right in the face.

Figure 1-4   The Winamp Player and Equalizer.

2. Load a test MP3 file (preferably one of your favorite songs) and click on the Play button on the transport controls of the Winamp Player. This will give you something to listen to (and an aural point of reference) while you are adjusting the level on the preamp and graphic EQ sliders.

3. Using the good taste that is second nature to you, gradually adjust the individual sliders in the Winamp EQ (remember, just because there are ten sliders doesn't mean you have to move them all) until you hear results that are pleasing to your ears. Just for aesthetic purposes, click the Preamp button to On and

slightly raise the Preamp slider up from zero dB. Notice that when you raise (or lower) the Preamp slider, the overall volume of the MP3 file you are listening to is affected. At this point, you now have a custom EQ setting.

4. Now to the true purpose of this tutorial — saving your custom EQ setting as a preset. On the Winamp Equalizer, select the Presets button (located in the top right-hand corner of the EQ window), and select Save and Preset as shown in Figure 1-5. Using Figure 1-6 as your reference, enter the name for your new preset as **test1,** and click the Save button to finish the process.

Figure 1-5   Select the Presets button on the Winamp Equalizer, and chose Save and Preset to open the Save EQ Preset dialog box.

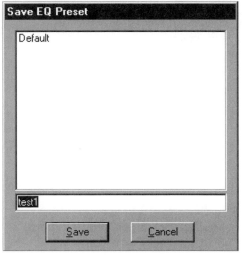

Figure 1-6   Name your EQ preset **test1,** and click the Save button.

Tutorial 1-1 Retrospect

Now that you know how to create and save an EQ/preamp preset, you are ready to review the range of what is available on the Presets menu.

Presets Menu

When you select the Presets button on the Winamp EQ, regardless of whether you select Load or Save, you are presented with four options: Preset, Auto-load preset, Default, and From/To EQF.

Because of your participation in Tutorial 1-1, you already know how to save an EQ preset, so it's time to address the how and why of the second option from the Presets+Save or Presets+Load menus, the *Auto-load preset*. While listening to a particular song, you can create a custom EQ/preamp setting. When you save the custom setting as an auto-load preset, the preset will automatically load whenever the song in question is played by the Winamp Player, providing you have engaged the Auto button on the Winamp EQ.

Your third option from the Presets+Save or Presets+Load menus is *Default*. By selecting Save+Default, you save your current preamp/EQ setting as the default. To recall your default setting from the Winamp EQ, select Presets +Load+Default.

Your fourth and final option from Presets menu is *From EQF*. From this menu, you can load an existing preset.

Creating Custom EQ Presets

There are no killer EQ/preamp settings that will work great for everyone. If we all used the same high-quality speaker system and had the same taste in music, then it would be a very boring world with a bunch of killer presets. Experiment, and you'll be able to create a few presets that will work well with your personal computer and speakers.

Winamp Plug-Ins

The Winamp Player has set the standard for plug-ins in the MP3 player arena. While the developers of other MP3 players are hard at work developing their own series of plug-ins for their respective players, for the time being the sheer number of plug-ins created by Winamp fans dwarf those of any other MP3 player we've come in contact with to date.

Note

If you haven't been there already, go to the Winamp plug-in page at the Nullsoft Web site: `www.winamp.com/plugins/index.html`.

Types of Plug-Ins

There are three different types of plug-ins for the Winamp Player: visualization, audio, and general. While plug-ins are great add-ons to any application, with the exception of a few of the visualization plug-ins, the majority of the Winamp plug-ins end up seeming sort of pointless. None of the audio effects plug-ins sounds all that great or serves any real purpose, and most mask the sound of the music. That's not a good thing. In defense of Winamp plug-ins, it is great that an open format exists and anyone with the skills and desire can create a unique plug-in and post it for all to see, hear, and/or use. The best thing for you to do is to form your own opinion by downloading and installing the Winamp plug-ins that fit your listening and visual needs.

Skins

When it comes to skins, Winamp is definitely on top. You can spend hours entertaining yourself with the many visualization possibilities afforded by Winamp skins. Some of you new to the MP3 phenomenon might not know what skins are. In the case of Winamp and some of the other MP3 players, a skin is just that — a visual skin that works as an alternative face, or front, of your MP3 player. While some of the older Winamp skins only worked on the Player portion of Winamp, there are now skins for the Winamp Equalizer and Playlist as well. For examples of skins, go online to `www.winamp.com/skins/index.html`, and click on Best Skins.

 ## Tutorial 1-2
CROSS-DRESSING WITH WINAMP SKINS

Just in case this whole skins thing has still got you baffled, here is a very simple tutorial that shows you just how easy it is to replace the standard Winamp look with a custom skin.

TOOLBOX

- Windows 95/98
- Most current version of Winamp (download it)

 On the Web

By going to www.mp3.com/order, you can purchase the MP3 Software Volume 1 CD-ROM and get over a thousand Winamp skins, plus rippers, encoders, and more software than there is space to mention. This will save you a lot of time and money.

1. Launch the application Winamp. Right click on the Options Menu button on the Winamp Player (refer back to Figure 1-1) and select Options+Skin Browser (or **Alt+S**), as shown in Figure 1-7, to open the Winamp Skin Browser window.

Figure 1-7   From the Options menu, select Options+Skin Browser.

2. The next step is to click the Set Skins Directory button in the Winamp Skin Browser window (refer to Figure 1-8) and choose the default file folder for your skins. To keep it simple, select the Skins folder in the Winamp folder as shown in Figure 1-9. Click the OK button to proceed.

Figure 1-8   The Winamp Skin Browser window.

Figure 1-9   Choose a default file folder as your skins directory.

3. For this step, make sure your computer is connected to the Internet. Click the Download Skins button (refer back to Figure 1-8) and, as if by magic, your computer will go directly to the Winamp Skins download page. Click on the link Best Skins and click the Download link on the skin of your choice. Download and save this file to the Winamp Skin Browser. Repeat until satisfied.

4. Close your Internet browser window, and in the Winamp Skin Browser select a skin (refer to Figure 1-10) and click the Close button. Your Winamp Player has now taken on the look of one of the many custom skins that reside in your Skins folder (see Figure 1-11).

Figure 1-10   Select a skin by clicking on it in the Winamp Skin Browser window.

Figure 1-11   The Winamp Player sporting a new look via the Spyamp skin.

Tutorial 1-2 Retrospect

The many Winamp skins are one of the best add-on features of the Winamp Player. It's fun to be able to change the look of the Player to fit your mood and the music. Some of these skins really look spectacular in color. You'll have to check that out for yourselves.

A Final Thought on Winamp

Nullsoft currently makes the claim that Winamp is the most downloaded MP3 player in the world. Many consider Winamp to be the best MP3 player on the planet, and for the time being this may be true. There's a lot of heavy competition coming down the pipeline, including (so the rumor says) a serious entry from Microsoft. Time will tell, but if the votes were cast today, Winamp would probably win the election without breaking a sweat.

SONIQUE

To date, the Sonique MP3 Player (www.sonique.com) from Night 55 is the best-looking player out there. While the Sonique Player (version .75) is still in a beta version, it's impressive how solid and crash-free this beta actually is. As far as sound quality goes, the Sonique Player seems to have a more natural uncolored sound than does the Winamp. When listening to music, the idea is to get as accurate a reproduction of the original recording as possible, and with the Sonique Player, the overall sound quality is as good as it gets with MP3. Okay, there's some of the nasty little bugs that pop up when using any beta software, but chances are that by the time you read this, Sonique will be out of beta anyway.

The Navigation Console

When you first boot the Sonique Player, you will see the main splash screen of the Navigation Console as shown in Figure 1-12. As you can see, the Navigation Console offers you six choices. While for the most part these options are self-explanatory, here's a quick tour.

Figure 1-12   The Sonique Navigation Console window gives you six navigation options: Online Tools, Playlist Editor, Enlarged Mode, Setup Options, Info About, and Audio Controls.

 Tip

Returning to the main screen of the Navigation Console is a very simple process if you know what to look for. Referring back to Figure 1-12, notice the four buttons in the top right-hand corner of the Navigation Console. Left to right, these are Minimize Player, Jump Down Once, Jump Down Twice, and Close Player, respectively. When you are in any of the Navigation Console options, a fifth button is added directly to the left of the other four (see Figure 1-13). To return to the Navigation Console, click this fifth button.

Online Tools

With the beta .75 release of the Sonique Player, all the links in the Online Tools window are up and running. Use the the links in the Online Tools window to get the latest information and updates for the Sonique Player (see Figure 1-14).

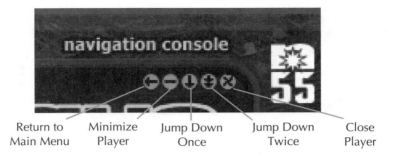

Figure 1-13   Click on the Return to Main Menu button to return to the main screen of the Navigation Console.

Figure 1-14   The Online Tools window of the Sonique Player.

Playlist Editor

The functions in the Sonique Playlist Editor are straightforward and easy to understand. Even the novice should have no problem figuring out how to use each of the individual functions in the Playlist Editor. Use Figure 1-15 and Table 1-4 as your reference to the different functions of the Sonique Playlist Editor. The only problem with the Playlist Editor is the lack of a drag-and-drop editing function to rearrange the order of files already in the list. Fortunately, you can load and play playlists created in Winamp and other applications. To create a custom playlist in the Sonique Playlist Editor, you need to load the songs one at a time in the order you plan to have them play. On the upside, remember this is beta and the issue will probably be addressed.

Figure 1-15   The Sonique Playlist Editor window.

Table 1-4   Sonique Playlist Editor Functions

Playlist Functions	Description
Sort	Sorts the files in playlist alphabetically.
Shuffle	Randomly shuffles the files in the playlist.
Reverse	Reverses the entire playlist.
Clear	Clears the entire playlist.
Add	Allows user to add either a file or playlist.
Remove	Removes either a selected MP3 file or the current playlist.
Save	Saves the current playlist as a file.

Enlarged Mode

The Enlarged Mode of the Sonique Player is the heart of its playback control (see Figure 1-16). Currently there are four visualization plug-ins that provide an incredible light show in the VU meter when music is playing. See Table 1-5 for an overview of the playback functions of the Sonique Player in the Enlarged Mode.

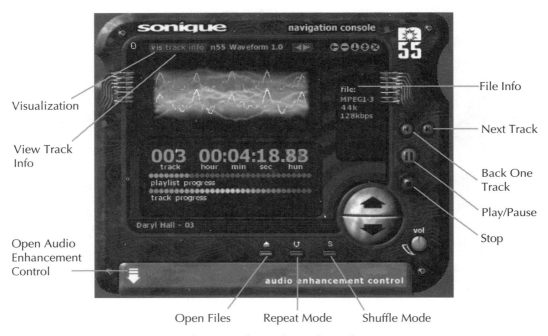

Figure 1-16   The Sonique Player in the Enlarged Mode.

 Note

The Sonique Player is also available in medium (see Figure 1-17) and small sizes. For the most part, the functionality is the same, and the player itself still has a unique look to it. To jump down in size to either the medium or small player, click either the Jump Down Once or Jump Down Twice button on the Sonique Player (refer back to Figure 1-13). These same buttons can also be used to restore the player to its enlarged status.

Table 1-5   Sonique Player Controls and Options

Function	Description
Visualization	Currently offers four different visual options in the VU section of the Player.
Track Info	Opens a window that allows the user to view track information from files in the playlist.
File Info	Lists the attributes of the file currently in play.
Next Track	Moves forward one track.
Back One Track	Moves back one track.
Play/Pause	Plays or pauses a track.
Stop	Stops playback of a track.
Audio Enhancement Control	Click anywhere on this bar to open the controls for the twenty-band graphic EQ as well as the amp (amplify decoder output), balance, and pitch controls.
Open Files	Opens MP3 and other supported audio and playlist files.
Repeat Mode	Loops a track or an entire playlist.
Shuffle Mode	Randomly shuffles the files in the playlist.

Figure 1-17   The medium-sized Sonique Player.

Setup Options

In the current version of Sonique (beta .75), the user has five different Setup Options menus. Table 1-6 provides a brief description of the functions in each of these menus.

Table 1-6   Sonique Setup Options

Function	Description
General	System options and playlist options.
Audio	Audio driver and audio buffer length.
Visual	System display performance.
File Type	Select (or deselect) the file types for playback on the Sonique Player.
Visual FX	Adjust the visual controls of the VU meter.

Info About

In the Info About section of the Navigation Console, you will find all the general information about the Sonique Player and development team. This includes recent bug fixes and general support information.

Audio Controls

The heart of the Sonique audio controls is the twenty-band graphic equalizer shown in Figure 1-18. The user has two control options: equalizer enabled and spline tension. The equalizer (EQ) must be enabled to hear the results of the spline tension function. With the spline tension function enabled, it is easier to create a more logical (and better sounding) waveform with the graphic EQ. In Figure 1-18, you can see a waveform created on the graphic EQ with spline tension enabled. The overall result is a much smoother waveform than what would have been created by adjusting one EQ slider at a time with the spline tension disabled. If you are confused about this whole EQ/spline tension thing, fire up your Sonique Player and experiment with the different features in the Audio Enhancement section of the Player.

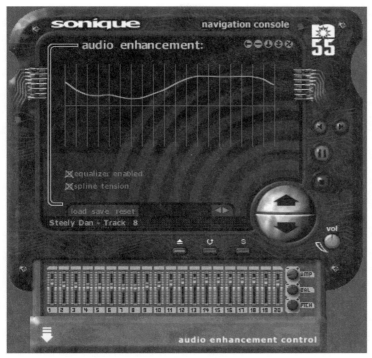

Figure 1-18 The Audio Enhancement section of the Sonique Player with the equalizer and spline tension enabled.

 Tip

If you are unfamiliar with how to use a graphic equalizer, refer back to Table 1-3 and to page 7 for some easy-to-understand basic information about graphic EQs in general.

 Note

At this time, Night 55 (the developer of the Sonique Player) is in the process of changing their name to Media-Science.

Sonique Retrospect

By the time the Sonique Player is out of beta and all the features are enabled, it is going to give Winamp a very serious run for its money. Currently, editing in the Playlist is pretty weak, and there are also a few minor functions that have yet to be brought online. It is a good-looking player, and the Sonique Player sounds really good, which is what counts. Currently, the Sonique Player is freeware and definitely worth trying out. Go to www.sonique.com and download the latest version. You won't regret it.

MUSICMATCH JUKEBOX 3.0

MusicMatch Jukebox 3.0 from Brava Software is one of the applications that you're going to see mentioned throughout this book. While one of its many functions is as an MP3 player, it is one of the few applications that can handle every aspect of managing your MP3 files. Besides being a full-functioned ripping and encoding package, it also serves as a database of MP3 files and a playlist editor. Some of you may still be using version 2.5 of this application. If this is the case, download the latest version of MusicMatch Jukebox 3.0, right now (www.musicmatch.com).

The Jukebox

The Player/Playlist window of MusicMatch Jukebox 3.0 (MMJB 3.0) has been dubbed by its creators the "Jukebox." Using Figure 1-19 and Table 1-7 as your reference, here is a basic overview of the Jukebox's functions. You will notice that unlike some MP3 players, the MMJB 3.0 transport controls are clearly marked and need no explanation.

 Tip

For those of you using the full version of MMJB 3.0, the Record (Rec) button found in the transport controls of the Jukebox can be used to open the ripping and encoding windows. For more on ripping and encoding with MMJB 3.0, go to Tutorial 4-3 in Chapter 4.

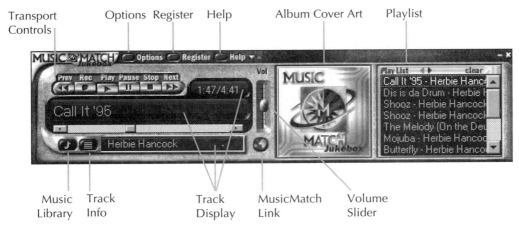

Figure 1-19   The MusicMatch Jukebox 3.0 MP3 player.

Table 1-7   The Jukebox

Function	Description
Options	Options Menu includes File, Edit, View, Player Controls, and Library Manager menus.
Register	Register, purchase, and update your copy of MMJB 3.0.
Help	Access the user's manual, online help, and other help-related functions of MMJB 3.0.
Transport Controls	Access playback and record functions.
Down/Up One Level	Shrink or expand the Jukebox.
Playlist	Organize files for playback.
Music Library Button	Open the Music Library.
Track Info Button	Access and edit track info on selected MP3 file.
Volume Slider	Volume control for the Jukebox.
Album Cover Art	Custom graphics can be displayed to fit either a promotion or a specific album. The user can also insert a custom graphic.
Track Display	Displays song name, artist, and time-elapsed information.
MusicMatch I-Music	Link to the MusicMatch I-Music Real Artists Web site.

More Jukebox Functions

As we mentioned, MusicMatch Jukebox is more than just a player. If you are new to the world of MP3, you may not be all that familiar with playlist management. Several of the tutorials in Chapter 2 deal with how to create and edit a playlist in different MP3-based applications, including MMJB 3.0. Also in Chapter 2, you'll learn how to edit an ID3 tag and add tons of information, such as lyrics and album liner notes, in the tag editing tutorials. Chapter 4 covers the ripping and encoding functions and features of MMJB 3.0, and last but not least, in Chapter 5, you'll find out how to use MMJB to export a playlist (or individual MP3 files) to the Rio Player.

For many of you, MusicMatch Jukebox 3.0 is going to give you everything you need to excel in the world of MP3. You can play and manage files with the Music Library and Playlist. You can also rip and encode CD audio to MP3, as well as edit and insert information that can be viewed while listening to your MP3 file. MusicMatch Jukebox would be a bargain at $50, and the fact that it's only $29.95 makes it that much better.

 On the Web

For the price of a free download, you can try out a demo version of MusicMatch Jukebox 3.0 (go to www.mp3.com/software/players.html). By purchasing the key from MusicMatch for $29.95, you can unlock all of the functions that make this application the true all-in-one MP3 application.

There are a lot of really great MP3 players (and applications) that are not featured in this book. There just isn't enough space or time to go in-depth with every player and application that is out there. Fortunately, by using the book, the MP3.com Web site, and the book's update pages (www.mp3.com/book/) as resources, you will have access to the latest information. Because the book's content can be updated on a weekly basis via the MP3.com Web site, your book will never be out of date. Where else can you get that kind of guarantee but at MP3.com?

HONORABLE MENTIONS

There are so many other really great MP3 players, it's hard to know where to start (or end). Be sure to check the Web site (www.mp3.com) for updates on all MP3 players. If we missed a player (or players) that you feel should have been featured in this chapter, contact Ron Simpson at `webaudioguru@excite.com`. Who knows, your observations may get you mentioned on the update pages for the book.

Unreal Player

Unreal Player from 303TEK (`www.303tek.com`) is an MP3 player with a five-star rating on MP3.com's Web site (see Figure 1-20). It is now in version 1.29, trial version 7. The cost of using Unreal Player seems to be $19.95, making it not that much of a bargain in comparison to Winamp or any of the other players you could get for free (or cheap).

Figure 1-20   Unreal Player version 1.29.

In terms of performance, first of all, the sound quality is pretty clean. There is no coloration of the sound of the MP3 file, and you get a close-to-CD-quality performance at 128 kbps (kilobytes per second). The Unreal Player is not the most intuitive unit, and there is a learning curve that may cause the average MP3 user to give up and use freeware or Winamp.

Unreal Player has a DJ function that allows you to create custom reverb and delay effects. As with several comparable Winamp audio effects plug-ins, the reverb and delay effects muddy up the sound and make the music sound worse, not better. The EQ is an easy edit and greatly improves the sound of the music. Finding the graphic EQ edit controls on the Unreal Player is sort of like going on a treasure hunt without the map. You need to do some right-clicking and will eventually get to the menu. Again, the technologically challenged would probably never figure out how to edit the EQ, while in Winamp or the Sonique Player they can get there easily.

If the Unreal Player cost in the area of $5 or $10, quite a few people might use it as an alternative to Winamp (or Sonique). At $19.95, however, not many people will use it past the initial thirty-day trial period. In spite of the steep learning curve, you will probably like it.

Windows Media Player

Windows Media Player (see Figure 1-21) is about as basic as you can get. With regards to the MP3 format, it will play either a single file or a playlist, and it does pseudo-streaming as well. As soon as an MP3 file starts to download, it will begin playing; it is not necessary for the entire file to have downloaded. If you have a slow connection or the Internet is clogged up with heavy traffic, the constant hiccups of the start and stop could get on your nerves.

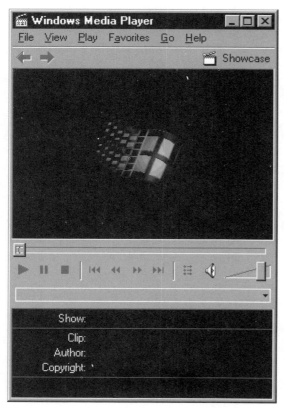

Figure 1-21   Windows Media Player 6.0.

The Windows Media Player 6.0 has all the charm and features of a basic everyday stripped-down car. The majority of Windows-based computer users will probably end up with Windows Media Player as their default MP3 player. It's there and it works.

 Note

Windows Media Player is a free download from Microsoft. Because the download page may move from place to place on Microsoft's Web site, here's how to find it. Go to Microsoft's home page (www.microsoft.com) and do a search for "Windows Media Player." This should link you to the proper download page within Microsoft's Web site.

 Tip

What happens whenever you download an MP3 file from the Web? Windows Media Player opens up and starts playing the file whether you like it or not . . . or does it? It's a matter of right-clicking the target link. By right-clicking the link and choosing Save Target As, you will be able to choose the destination folder of the MP3 file that you plan on downloading, and it won't start to play back during the downloading process.

FreeAmp

When the development world adds functionality to FreeAmp Player 1.0 (see Figure 1-22), it will be able to go head-to-head with most of the MP3 players that are currently available, but right now it's just not up to par. It does sound great, and you can load random MP3 files into the FreeAmp Player. But beyond that, the only other controls are Volume and Seek — the Playlist is still a disabled function in version 1.0. Be sure to check the update pages (www.mp3.com/book/), and as more functionality and features are added to FreeAmp, we'll let you know about them.

Figure 1-22   FreeAmp 1.0.

MACINTOSH

When it comes to dedicated MP3 players and the Mac, the choices are few and far between. The MP3 revolution is for the most part a Windows thing. MacAmp (1.0b7) is in a beta version, and it is the first Mac-based player covered here.

 On the Web

Go to `www.mp3.com/software/mac/players.html` to download the latest version of MacAmp.

MacAmp

MacAmp (`www.macamp.com`) seems quite similar to its Windows counterparts, and yet very Mac-like. This is a good thing. It's possible to create a lot of Winamp-like custom features for MacAmp, and there are some very cool MacAmp skins. Unlike their sometimes quirky Windows counterparts, MacAmp plug-ins are easy to install and use. Like it's distant Windows cousin Winamp, MacAmp comes with essentially three components: the Player, the Equalizer, and the Playlist.

The Player

The MacAmp Player has a very generic, almost minimalistic look to it, and the controls border on being idiot-proof. Using Figure 1-23 for reference, you can see that the transport controls (Play/Pause, Repeat, Shuffle, and Volume Control) are all conveniently located along the bottom of the Player.

 Note

MacAmp users have two separate options for making the Player controls, EQ, and Playlist visible or invisible. From the MacAmp Windows pull-down menu you can actually toggle the Player, EQ, and Playlist between visible and invisible. This can also be accomplished by selecting **Command+1** for the Player, **Command+2** for the EQ, and **Command+3** for the Playlist.

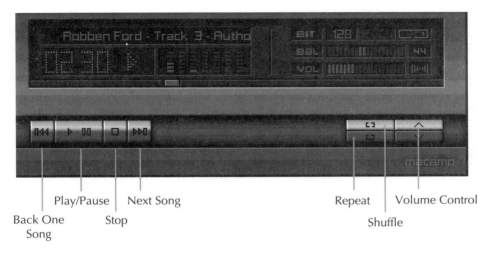

Play/Pause | Next Song   Repeat | Volume Control

Back One   Stop   Shuffle
  Song

Figure 1-23   The MacAmp Player.

The Equalizer

The second MacAmp component is an eight-band graphic equalizer (see Figure 1-24). Currently, the only way to save an EQ setting in the MacAmp Equalizer is by saving the EQ setting along with the volume, pan information, and songs into a playlist. When you open the saved playlist, all of this information (including the EQ settings) is recalled. The EQ can also be anchored to (or set free from) the Player by toggling **Command+E**. This is to ensure that both components travel together when moved around the desktop. The Equalizer can also be made visible or invisible by toggling **Command+3**.

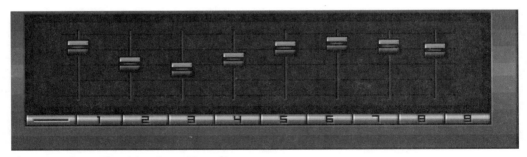

Figure 1-24   The MacAmp Equalizer.

The Playlist

Using Figure 1-25 as your reference, notice there are four function buttons in the MacAmp Playlist. You can add or delete as well as open or close files or playlists using the various buttons. With MacAmp, it is also possible to open playlists that were created with Winamp or other Windows-based playlist editors. In Chapter 2, we'll go through the basics of how to create and manage playlists, including the MacAmp Playlist.

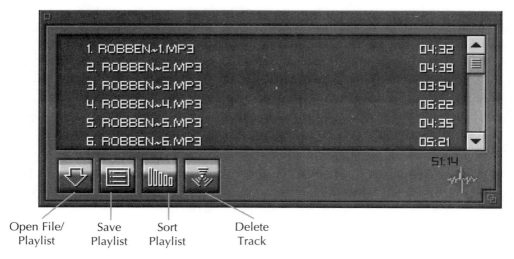

Figure 1-25   The MacAmp Playlist.

MacAmp Is . . .

MacAmp comes off as conservative and minimalistic in comparison with Windows MP3 players. While this is not really a bad thing, most of us expect the Macintosh side of the fence to have more of an outlaw mentality than the PC side, but this time the shoe is on the other foot (so to speak). Nonetheless, the MacAmp Player is worthy of being the default MP3 player for the Mac.

Other Mac Players

Another Mac-based freeware application that will play MP3 files is SoundApp. Developed by Norman Franke (a recent Stanford graduate), SoundApp is available as a free download from his Stanford home page (the URL is in the list at the end of the chapter). SoundApp is actually more than just an MP3 player and is compatible with quite a few common (and not so common) file formats.

The AudioActive MP3 player (www.audioactive.com) from Telos is another no-frills freeware MP3 player. What makes this player unique is that when you encounter certain types of streaming MP3 (those that originate from the Telos MP3 servers), you can experience true streaming MP3 over the Web.

CHAPTER RETROSPECT

At the time of this writing, Winamp is the most downloaded and used MP3 player on the planet. It will be interesting to see what's going to shake out when the Sonique Player makes it out of beta.

COMING UP . . .

In Chapter 2, we'll look at managing MP3 files by using a playlist. Also, where do you find MP3 files on the Web? By using a combination of Chapter 2 and the Chapter 2 update Web page (www.mp3.com/book/), you will be able to find the best places to download both free and commercial MP3 files.

 On the Web

Here's a quick list of where you can find the different MP3 players featured in this chapter:

Winamp: www.winamp.com
Sonique: www.sonique.com
MusicMatch Jukebox: www.musicmatch.com
Unreal Player: www.303tek.com
Windows Media Player: www.microsoft.com
FreeAmp: www.freeamp.com
MacAmp: www.macamp.com
SoundApp: www-cs-students.stanford.edu/~franke/SoundApp/
AudioActive: www.audioactive.com

Go to www.mp3.com/software/players.html to find download links to just about every MP3 player on the planet.

2

Finding and Playing MP3s

If it's easier to find and buy the legal stuff, it greatly reduces the demand for the illegal stuff. I challenge anyone to find drug dealers pushing aspirin. Why would anyone frequent a drug dealer when aspirin is prevalent, cheap, and high-quality? Making music as prevalent as aspirin and "one click easy" for netters to buy is the most significant step the music business can take to combat piracy.

— *Michael Robertson*

IN THIS CHAPTER

- Finding MP3 Files
- Playlists
- File Management
- Archiving
- SHOUTcast

Those of you who are new to the world of MP3 and maybe even the Internet may need a little help locating some MP3 files for playback. In the first section of this chapter, we're going to help you do just that. When it comes down to it, there are essentially three types of MP3 files you are going to find on the Web.

First off, there are the legal MP3 files that are posted by musicians and record companies as a way to help promote their music. The second option is e-commerce, in which the artist or company sells digital downloads to the end user. While there is currently no price standard, most downloadable digital music will probably cost between $1 and $2 per track. The third and last way to obtain MP3 files is from so-called pirate Web sites. We do not recommend that you search out and download music from the pirate sites — they threaten the integrity of the industry.

On the Web

This is one of those instances where the combination of this book and the update Web site will come in very handy. Go straight to MP3.com (www.mp3.com/book/) and check the Chapter 2 update page. This is where you'll be able to find a current list of the best MP3 Web sites for downloadable MP3 files. Also remember that MP3.com has more than a thousand free (and legal) MP3 files that are just a download away.

FINDING MP3 ACTION ON THE WEB

The rest of the planet is beginning to discover what we already know — MP3 is changing the music world and how we listen to music. Previewing music with MP3 is better for both the buyer and the seller. As consumers, we can choose what and who we listen to, and our options are not limited to what our local retailer carries or has in stock. On the Web, the spectrum of artists can range from a neighborhood garage band to the latest Grammy Award winner. And if by chance we like what we hear, we can simply click on a link and purchase a CD or downloadable MP3 track. This is a win-win situation for both consumers and recording artists.

 Tip

For you Windows users out there who have downloaded an MP3 file or two off of the Web, you might have noticed that the Windows Media Player 6.0 tends to pop up and start playing whenever you start downloading an MP3. You can avoid this sometimes painful intrusion by right-clicking the target link (instead of left-clicking it). In this way, you can just save the file and listen to it at your leisure (and with the MP3 player of choice), rather than have it start playing without your permission.

MP3.com

Even if this book weren't titled *The Official MP3.com Guide to MP3*, the MP3.com Web site would still be the first recommended stop for anyone interested in the MP3 phenomenon. If you were wondering where to find links to many thousands of free (and legal) MP3 files, then wonder no more. Just about the first thing you see when you arrive at MP3.com is the "Free" heading (see Figure 2-1).

There is a different featured song of the day, and you can also locate artists and music according to genre. Besides promotional MP3 files from a number of name artists, yet-to-be-discovered musicians and songwriters are featured on the MP3.com Web site — literally thousands of them!

The
Free Music
Link

Figure 2-1   By going to www.mp3.com and clicking the "Free" link, you can download more than a thousand MP3 files.

MP3.com is the first MP3-related Web site that many of us visit, and it is often the first place we look (and listen) when going online. Unlike many other Web sites, it is well-designed, making it easy to find the free music downloads.

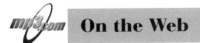 **On the Web**

If you're not sure where to begin but want to hear a lot of music, the solution is the MP3.com *Music CD*. By going to www.mp3.com/order, you can purchase a CD sampler containing over 150 CD-quality songs from musicians on the verge of being discovered.

MusicMatch

In addition to selling the all-in-one MusicMatch Jukebox, MusicMatch (www.musicmatch.com) is one of the best resources on the Internet with free full-length promotional MP3 files. With the exception of MP3.com, there isn't another Web site that offers easy access to this many legal full-length MP3 files at no cost to the consumer.

Another good way to beef up your MP3 collection is to buy the *Best of Independent American Music*. This CD-ROM was jointly developed by MusicMatch and songs.com and contains 152 CD-quality MP3 tracks. When listening to the contents of the CD using the MusicMatch Jukebox, you can also view the cover art, lyrics, and bios of the individual artists. If you just can't wait, there is also a Pay Music section on the MusicMatch Web site, where you can preview songs in RealAudio and purchase individual MP3 downloads. If you are interested in hearing CD-quality MP3 previews from a wide selection of independent artists, the MusicMatch Web site should be added to your online itinerary.

GoodNoise

GoodNoise (www.goodnoise.com) bills itself as *the* Internet record company, and they are doing a good job of living up to the claim. The free MP3 files available at the GoodNoise Web site run the gamut from thirty-second demos to full-length promo tracks of original music. GoodNoise also offers entire albums for sale as MP3 downloads. This is great for the consumer and is sort of bucking the trend of waiting for some type of standardized MP3 copy protection to hit the mainstream. Unfortunately, you probably won't find content from many mainstream pop artists available for sale as MP3 tracks yet. Until the Recording Industry Association of America (RIAA) and the record industry in general come to a consensus on what the acceptable digital delivery form will be, we consumers will continue previewing and purchasing music from online pioneers such as MP3.com and GoodNoise. GoodNoise is another example of an Internet music company that is leading the way to the future of online music.

 Note

SDMI, the Secure Digital Music Initiative, is a creation of the RIAA, whose purpose is to create a set of industry-wide standards for selling secure downloadable digital music. At this writing, it is too early to know what effect SDMI will have on the world of MP3.

PlatinumCD.com

PlatinumCD.com (`www.platinumcd.com`) offers free promotional MP3 tracks in varying lengths (thirty seconds and more) as well as RealAudio previews of featured artists. One of the services offered by PlatinumCD.com is called "Create (your own) Custom CD." For those of you without CD-burning capabilities, this is an invaluable way to create your own best-hits CD. You can take delivery of this CD as a download to your computer, or PlatinumCD.com will have it delivered to your door. As you can imagine, this opens up some interesting possibilities for the future of music delivery.

MP3 Search Engines

If you're not sure what you're looking for, or you have a vague idea and you're wondering if it's available in the MP3 format, there are a number of search engines devoted to locating sites with MP3 files. Search engines can save lots of headaches when it comes to wading through the muck of the World Wide Web.

RioPort.com

In November 1998, the release of Diamond Multimedia's Rio Player sent shudders through the record industry that have yet to subside. With the launch of RioPort.com (`www.rioport.com`), MP3 users have access to an online search engine that finds only legal MP3 files. RioPort.com is definitely a step toward legitimizing the MP3 movement. RioPort includes a lot of legitimate options for finding MP3 files and unlike some other search engines, it doesn't contain outdated links. In the opening months of 1999, Diamond Multimedia's RioPort.com is one of the best online search resources for finding legitimate MP3 files on the Web.

Lycos

"Seek and you will find" would be a good way to describe the new Lycos MP3 search engine (`mp3.lycos.com`). Go there, enter the artist or song name, click on the Go Get It button, and in no time a series of links will appear. So does it work? That's hard to answer. When we tested the site in its first weeks of operation, it was easy to generate links. But downloading MP3 files was a different story. Some of them (which were probably illegal) had been removed from the server. In one case, we were kicked off of a site because too many visitors were overloading the capacity of the server. When it came to trying to download an

MP3 file in the category of popular music, we struck out. We had better luck in the world of deceased jazz musicians, but not much. By then, the Lycos MP3 search engine had become so popular that it was difficult to connect to the Lycos Web site at all. Lycos is the first major portal site to offer a dedicated MP3 search engine. Our experience is an indicator of how popular MP3 is becoming.

MP3.com

Go to `www.mp3.com/search.html` if you really want to consolidate your resources. Thanks to MP3.com, you can link to multiple MP3 search engines. If you're not able to find it here, it isn't anywhere.

 On the Web

With regards to MP3 and the Internet, nothing will remain static for very long. It seems like every week there is a major shake-up, stuff changes, and new resources become available. As part of our commitment to keeping this book current, we will be updating the content of each chapter on the Web. By going to `www.mp3.com/book/` you will be able to find new links, updated content, and general information.

CREATING A PLAYLIST

The heart of any great MP3 player is the Playlist. The Playlist allows you to add, delete, rearrange, and save a series of songs into an easy-to-retrieve file. Some MP3 players take things a step farther and allow the user to save Volume, Balance, and EQ settings along with the Playlist. While no two MP3 players deal with playlists in exactly the same manner, once you learn the basic concepts, you should have no trouble creating custom playlists using any capable MP3 player.

 Note

Playlists created on one player will open on some other players:

1. The Sonique Player opened and played a Winamp Playlist.
2. MusicMatch Jukebox 3.0 opens only Playlists created on the MMJB itself.
3. Unreal Player opened and played a Winamp Playlist.

4. Windows Media Player 6.0 opened and played a Winamp Playlist, but no ID3 tag information was displayed.

5. FreeAmp 1.0 does not support playback via playlists.

6. MacAmp 1.0b7 will not load or recognize a playlist (an M3U file) that was created in Winamp.

The Playlist Tutorials

To date, the most popular MP3 player on the Windows platform is Winamp. For the Macintosh it is MacAmp. Therefore, the following tutorials use the Winamp (www.winamp.com) and MacAmp (www.macamp.com) Players. Because MusicMatch Jukebox 3.0 is such a popular all-in-one system, there is a playlist tutorial for the MMJB in the section called "File Management" immediately following the Winamp and MacAmp Playlist tutorials.

Tutorial 2-1
CREATING A WINAMP PLAYLIST

You've just downloaded the latest version of the Winamp Player (www.winamp.com) and you were also able to find some legal MP3 downloads at MP3.com. By creating a custom playlist, you can hear the music you want to hear in the order you want to hear it by simply loading one file.

TOOLBOX

- Two or more MP3 files (preferably five)
- The latest version of Winamp
- A Pentium computer running Windows 95/98, NT 4.0 (or better)

Let's Get Started

For this tutorial, we're going to take five different MP3 files and create a custom playlist. Because in theory you only need two MP3 files to make a playlist, you may use as many or as few MP3 files as you want. Also, before you start this tutorial, make sure that you have the MP3 files that you will use stashed in a folder somewhere.

1. Open the application Winamp and click either the PL button on the Winamp Player (see Figure 2-2 for reference) or **Alt+E** to open the Playlist Editor.

2. In this step, you need to move your target MP3 files into the Playlist Editor. Click the +File button located in the lower left-hand corner of the Winamp Playlist Editor window (refer to Figure 2-2). In the resulting window, locate the folder in which you've saved your MP3 files, and select the target files you wish to load into the playlist (as shown in Figure 2-3). In this case, select all five MP3 files and click Open. This loads the five target MP3 files into the Winamp Playlist Editor.

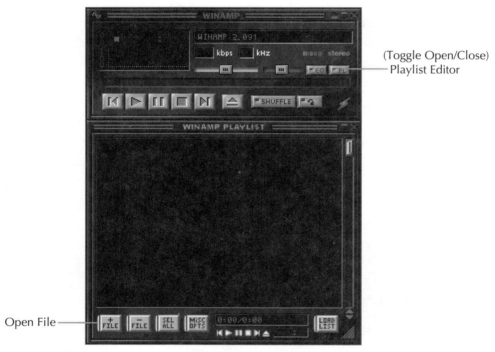

Figure 2-2   Click the PL button (or **Alt+E**) on the Winamp Player to open the Winamp Playlist Editor.

 Tip

Opening multiple files (instead of one at a time) can save you a lot of time. As in all Windows applications, you can use the **Ctrl** key to select random files, or the **Shift** key to select a group of files. Then, click the Open button, and all selected files are loaded into the Playlist.

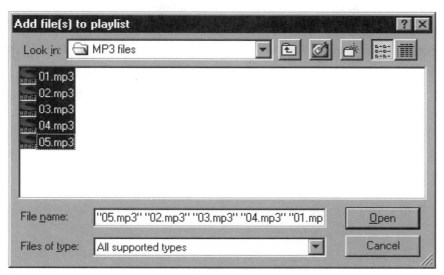

Figure 2-3   Select the target files you wish to load into the Playlist.

3. Now that the MP3 files are sitting in the Winamp Playlist Editor, let's say that you would like to change the order of play before saving the files into a single playlist. Select the file you wish to move by clicking on it once. In this case, select Track 5, as shown in Figure 2-4.

Figure 2-4   Select Track 5 by clicking on it in the Playlist Editor.

4. To move the target file to its new location, again click on the file you have
    selected (Track 5), hold the left mouse button down, and drag the file to its new
    location, for example, to the second position in the Playlist (as shown in Figure
    2-5). Regardless of the size of your playlist, you can drag the files around and
    listen to them in any order you wish. Other sorting options will be covered at
    the end of this tutorial.

Figure 2-5   Note that Track 5 now resides in the second position in the Playlist
Editor.

5. Now all that is left to do is save this list of songs into a playlist. At the bottom
    right-hand corner of the Winamp Playlist Editor is a button named Load List
    (refer to Figure 2-5 for reference). Right-click the Load List button (or use
    Ctrl+S) and select Save Playlist. This opens the Save Playlist window. Under
    File name, enter **test1** and under Save as type, choose M3U Playlist (as shown
    in Figure 2-6). To finish this tutorial, click the Save button. You have now creat-
    ed your first playlist, **test1 (.M3U)**.

 Tip

The Winamp Playlist Editor has a few slick sorting functions you should be aware
of. At the bottom of the Winamp Playlist Editor, there is a button called Misc Opts
(it's the fourth button from the left). Click this button, and select Sort List to get five
different sorting options (refer to Figure 2-7). Select any one of these five options to
sort the files that reside in the Playlist Editor.

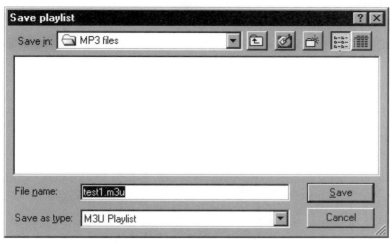

Figure 2-6   Enter the File name, Save as type, and then click Save.

Figure 2-7   Each of the five different sorting options for the Winamp Playlist Editor is self-explanatory.

Tutorial 2-1 Retrospect

As you can see, creating and saving a custom playlist with the Winamp Playlist Editor is a simple and intuitive process. What types of and how many songs you put into a playlist is completely a personal call. The playlist itself does not house the MP3 files, but instead acts as a link to them. If you remove an MP3 file from your hard drive and try to recall it through an active playlist, you will be completely out of luck.

Tutorial 2-2
CREATING A MACAMP PLAYLIST

If you are a hard-core Mac user, you probably feel as though your platform of choice has been largely ignored by the MP3 revolution that has been sweeping the planet. At the time of this writing, the beta version of MacAmp is the only Mac-based MP3 player that offers Windows-like features, such as skins, plug-ins, and a playlist with editing. This situation will probably change in the near future. This tutorial will show you the basics of building and editing a MacAmp Playlist.

TOOLBOX

- Two or more MP3 files (preferably five)
- The latest version of MacAmp (go to www.macamp.com to download it)
- A Power Macintosh running System 7.6 (or better)

Let's Get Started

1. Start MacAmp, and from the Windows pull-down menu select Playlist (or **Command+2**) to open the MacAmp Playlist Editor. As you can see in Figure 2-8, the MacAmp Player, Equalizer (EQ), and Playlist Editor will all be visible.

 Note

Using the **Command** (Apple) key on the keyboard, you can toggle each of the three components of the MacAmp Player between visible and invisible. For the Player, use **Command+1**, for the Equalizer **Command+2**, and for the Playlist Editor **Command+3**. When an MP3 file or playlist is playing and you toggle each or all of the three MacAmp components to their invisible status, the files will continue to play.

2. Move your target MP3 files into the MacAmp Playlist Editor. The easiest way to accomplish this task is to drag and drop the files anywhere on the Player, EQ, or Playlist Editor (they will end up in the Playlist Editor). Your other option is to load the target MP3 files one at a time via the File pull-down menu (File+Open).

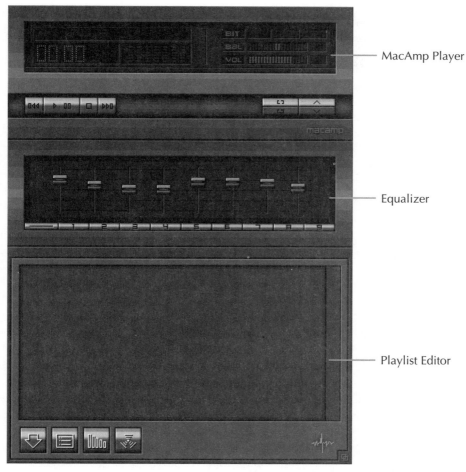

MacAmp Player

Equalizer

Playlist Editor

Figure 2-8   The three components of MacAmp are the MacAmp Player, Equalizer, and Playlist Editor.

3. As you can see in Figure 2-9, there are now five MP3 files in the MacAmp Playlist Editor. Select Track 5 by clicking on it once, and then, while holding the mouse button, drag it to the second position in the Playlist as shown in Figure 2-10.

4. The fourth and final step is to save this combination of MP3 files as a playlist. Click the Save Playlist button (refer to Figure 2-10) to open the Save Playlist as window. Name the playlist **test1**, and click the Save button.

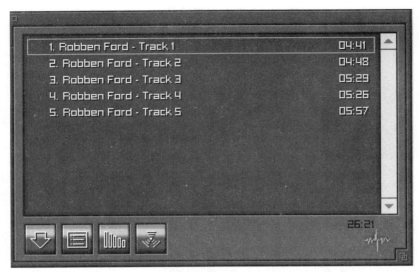

Figure 2-9   The five target MP3 tracks in the MacAmp Playlist Editor.

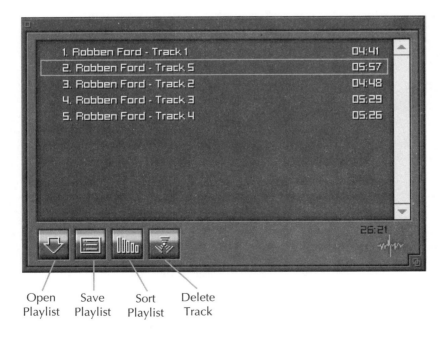

Figure 2-10   Click and drag Track 5 to the second position in the Playlist.

Tutorial 2-2 Retrospect

There's a cool playlist option in MacAmp: Each song can have a custom EQ setting within a playlist. When that particular song is played, the MacAmp EQ defaults to the saved EQ setting. Here's how to turn this function on. From the MacAmp pull-down menu, select Edit+Preferences+Playlist and enable the checkbox Store song volume, panning and EQs in the playlist as shown in Figure 2-11. Click the OK button to exit back to the MacAmp Player. As you can see from the Playlist Preferences window in Figure 2-11, there are a number of other options you can enable or disable.

Check This Box

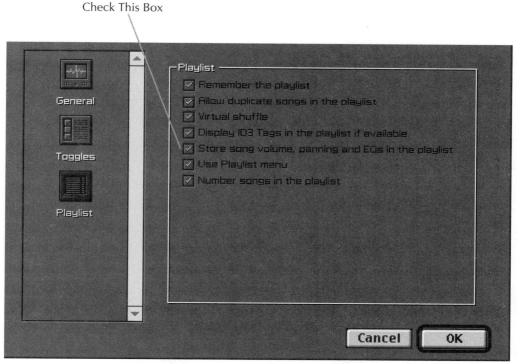

Figure 2-11   By enabling the checkbox Store song volume, panning and EQs in the playlist, all of these settings are automatically stored when you save a playlist.

Before We Move On

When it comes down to it, creating, editing, and saving a playlist is pretty easy stuff. In the next section, we'll give you a few ideas on how you can manage all those MP3 and playlist files that are starting to clutter up your computer.

FILE MANAGEMENT

Essentially, there are two simple ways to organize an MP3 collection: Build your own directory, or use the Music Library component of MusicMatch Jukebox (MMJB 3.0). The Music Library is by far a better way to go.

Tutorial 2-3
UTILIZING THE MMJB 3.0 MUSIC LIBRARY

Before you can work through this tutorial, you need to purchase the full version of MusicMatch Jukebox 3.0. Go to www.musicmatch.com/jukebox/, and download and install the free demo version. Then follow the instructions to upgrade to the full version.

 On the Web

You are also going to need some MP3 files to complete this tutorial. If you don't already have some, go to www.mp3.com and click on the Free link. From there, choose and download a few MP3 files and place them in the Music folder in the main MMJB 3.0 folder.

 Note

MusicMatch Jukebox 3.0 is also a full-featured CD ripper and MP3 encoder. CD ripping software digitally extracts an audio file (or files) from an audio CD. In the case of Windows computers, the ripped file becomes a WAVE file. The MP3 encoder is what converts the WAVE file into an MP3 file. In Tutorial 4-3 (Chapter 4), you will learn how easy it is to use MMJB 3.0 for one-step ripping and encoding.

TOOLBOX

- Three or more MP3 files
- MusicMatch Jukebox 3.0 (full version)
- A Pentium computer running Windows 95/98 or NT 4.0 (or better)

1. Open MusicMatch Jukebox 3.0 and click the Open Music Library button on the Jukebox (see Figure 2-12 for reference).

Open Music Library

Figure 2-12   Open the Music Library by clicking the Open Music Library button on MMJB 3.0.

2. Now that the Music Library window is open (see Figure 2-13), you need to add the target MP3 files to the database. Click the Add button on the Music Library, and open the file folder holding the target MP3 files as shown in Figure 2-14. Because you want to move all of the MP3 files from the folder Music into the Music Library, click Select All and OK to complete the process.

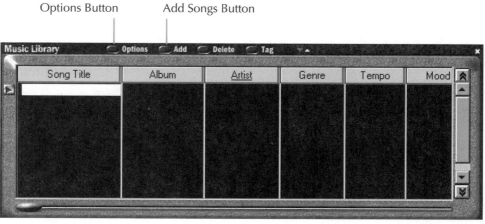

Options Button   Add Songs Button

Figure 2-13   Click the Add button on the Music Library to open the Add Songs window.

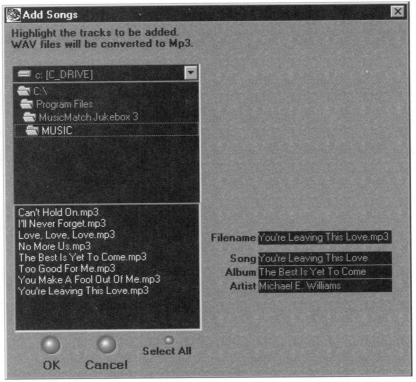

Figure 2-14   Click Select All and OK to load all the MP3 files into the Music Library.

 Note

You can use the database in the Music Library in a variety of different ways. For example, you can sort songs by artist and album, then use the Add Songs feature to build custom database files within the Music Library.

3. To save the contents of the Music Library, click the Options button on the Music Library (refer back to Figure 2-13), select Save As, name the file **TEST1.MMD**, and click Save.

4. While looking at the Music Library, select three songs you would like to move into the Playlist. You have two choices in method of transport: drag and drop, or just double-click on a song in the Music Library. To complete this tutorial step, double-click each of the three songs you have selected. You should now have the three songs in the MMJB Playlist, as shown in Figure 2-15.

Options Button

Figure 2-15   By double-clicking on MP3 files in the Music Library, you can add them to the MMJB 3.0 Playlist.

5. To save the three songs as a playlist, click the Options button (refer to Figure 2-15) on the Jukebox and select File+Save Playlist. This opens the Saving Playlist dialog box. Enter the filename **Test2**, and click the OK button (Figure 2-16).

Figure 2-16   Enter the filename **Test2** and click OK to save the Playlist.

Tutorial 2-3 Retrospect

You can add the contents of one or many CDs to the Music Library and save the CDs as single, easy-to-retrieve MMD files. You can also add many songs (MP3 files) to the MMJB Playlist simply by double-clicking them in the Music Library. You can add songs from multiple database files into a single playlist and save that playlist separately. This is nice if you organize and save your MMD files by artist and CD. Each of you will probably come up with a different method of organizing your MP3 files. If you have come up with any innovative tips and tricks in this regard, send Ron Simpson an e-mail; time and space permitting, we will post it on the book update Web page.

ARCHIVING

At some point, you're going to fill up your computer's hard drive with MP3 files. Your best bet is to archive your excess MP3s to some form of removable media. Here's a quick look at a few popular and reasonably priced archiving solutions.

Iomega

At this stage of the game, the battle to see who would control the market of affordable removable media has been won hands-down by Iomega (www.iomega.com). The original Zip drives and disks offer 100 MB of storage. There is also a newer, more powerful Zip drive that offers 250 MB of storage per disk and reads the older 100 MB Zip disks as well.

The Iomega Jazz drive offers one or two gigabytes of removable storage. But most of you probably won't want to spend $100 or more per disk to archive your MP3 files.

There's also a new kid on the block, and it is likely that the newly released Iomega Clic drives and disks are going to become the removable/recordable choice of the MP3 generation. There are a couple of reasons for this. First off, the 40 MB Clic disks are small and easy to handle, and the Clic drives are fairly portable as well. Second and more important is the VaroMan Plus from Varo Vision (www.varovision.com). This is a multifunction device that operates as an MP3 player, digital voice recorder, and personal organizer. It features a built-in Iomega Clic drive that allows the user to transfer MP3 files from a computer, via the Clic disks, and it also comes with a parallel port connector for transferring data from a computer. In Chapter 5, we'll take you on an in-depth tour of the portable MP3 devices currently (or soon to be) available.

Going to CD

Now that a blank CD costs less than $2, archiving your MP3 files to CD-ROM is by far the most logical and cost-effective storage solution currently available. With up to 650 MB of available storage per CD, it is possible to save about 650 minutes of MP3 music (encoded at 128 kbps) on one $2 CD. Not a bad deal, no matter how you look at it. Some CD-ROM burners are selling for under $300, including software. To check out compatibility and general info on CD burners, refer to the MP3.com Web site for the latest updated information on the hardware: www.mp3.com/hardware/cdr.html.

Whether you use Mac or Windows computers, if you have a CD-ROM burner you are probably using software created and sold by Adaptec (www.adaptec.com). Most popular CD-burning hardware packages are bundling either Adaptec's Toast (for Macintosh) or Easy CD Creator (for Windows). While there are other software options for making your own CDs, these applications seem to have become the unofficial standard for creating your own CDs.

Adaptec Toast (Mac)

With Toast, you are not limited to creating content just for the Mac. You can create a Mac/Windows hybrid CD that works flawlessly. You can also make a Windows-only CD-ROM or a CD-ROM that will also function as an audio CD. It's possible to create CDs that consist of any and all combinations of Mac, Windows, and audio data.

If you are a Mac user and you need to archive your MP3 files (or any other data files), use Toast. In fact, Toast works so well that recording studios use it to make reference audio CDs for their clients.

Adaptec Easy CD Creator

The latest version of Easy CD Creator Deluxe Edition 3.5 for Windows (also from Adaptec) offers a lot of features beyond archiving MP3 files. Not only can you burn an audio or data CD with this application, there is also a jewel case layout function as well. This allows the user to create custom CD covers and more. CD Copier Deluxe enables you to make copies of any audio CD. CD Spin Doctor enables you to record, edit, and apply special effects processes to the target audio files.

 On the Web

Easy CD Creator is just that — easy. Using the Wizard, even a beginner could archive and burn their MP3 files without any problems. However, if this is not the case, a tutorial will be available on the update pages at MP3.com (www.mp3.com/book).

Regardless of your skill level, this application offers a lot of bang for the buck and is bundled with many of the CD-ROM burners being sold today. In short, if you are a Windows user and are planning to archive your MP3 (or data) files to CD-ROM, use Easy CD Creator.

SHOUTCAST

Well, it looks like Justin and the Nullsoft development team have done it again. SHOUTcast makes it possible for anyone with a Windows computer, a modem, and audio content to originate an MP3 streaming broadcast. RealNetworks currently charges $25,000 to license four hundred streams of audio and video via the RealServer, and that is just the licensing fee. If you put RealAudio up against MP3 in a sound-quality comparison, MP3 will win hands-down. SHOUTcast is a real breakthrough. Some computer experts have said that there really isn't anything to streaming MP3 and that SHOUTcast is a resource hog. While this may or may not be true, SHOUTcast audio sounds good.

Tutorial 2-4
USING SHOUTCAST

Using SHOUTcast is a simple process. The results are going to vary based upon your computer, modem, and the speed and reliability of your Internet connection. The amount of RAM available in your computer will probably have some bearing on what you hear. Those connecting to the Internet with ADSL, cable modem, or another high-speed connection will probably enjoy near flawless performance even when listening to MP3 streams at 128 kbps. Those using a dial-up will have better luck listening to the SHOUTcast broadcasts that stream at a lower bit rate.

TOOLBOX

- The latest version of Winamp (go to `www.winamp.com` to get it)
- Browser: Internet Explorer 4 (or better) or Netscape Navigator 4.0 (or better)
- A Pentium computer running Windows 95/98 or NT 4.0 (or better), connected to the Internet

Note

Before you start this tutorial, it is necessary to configure the Winamp Player to automatically deal with PLS files. Start the Winamp application, and select **Ctrl+P** to open the Winamp preferences. Click on the Setup tab, and under Extensions, select pls. Click Apply and OK.

1. Log on to the Internet, go to www.shoutcast.com, and click the Listen link in the Navigation bar to go to the SHOUTcast directory. Your goal in this step is to choose which SHOUTcast you are going to listen to. There are two options: TOP 10 SHOUTCASTS (see Figure 2-17) and the currently running SHOUTcasts as listed by genre.

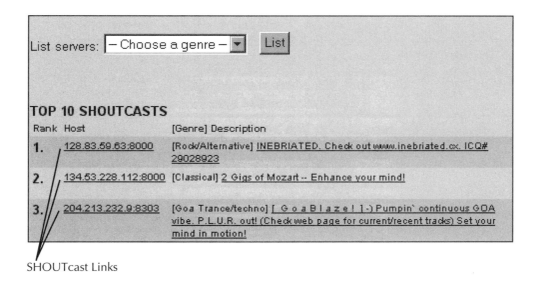

SHOUTcast Links

Figure 2-17   Choose a SHOUTcast either by genre or from the TOP 10 SHOUTCASTS, then click the link, sit back, and listen.

2. Once you have chosen which SHOUTcast you want to listen to, click the link under Host (refer to Figure 2-17) to start the SHOUTcast. You will be asked if you want to open the incoming information or save it to disk. Choose Open, and in a few seconds you will be listening to your first SHOUTcast.

Tutorial 2-4 Retrospect

The most common problem using SHOUTcast is that you click on a SHOUTcast link and nothing happens. It is possible you may have to enter the URL manually. Select **Ctrl+L** in Winamp to get the Winamp Open Location dialog box to pop up (Figure 2-18). You then manually enter the URL and click Open to start a SHOUTcast. The URL of each featured SHOUTcast is listed under Host in the SHOUTcast directory (refer back to Figure 2-17 and steps 1 and 2 of Tutorial 2-4).

Figure 2-18   An alternate way to play a SHOUTcast from Winamp is to enter the URL manually. Select **Ctrl+L** to access the Open Location dialog box in Winamp.

Another small problem is the dreaded streaming hiccup: When there's net congestion, when your ISP can't handle the bandwidth, or when the host server has too many requests for data streams, the content you are listening to starts to hiccup and cut out. With the SHOUTcast server, if the amount of available streams is set higher than the bandwidth can actually process and too many people are attempting to listen, your online radio reception starts to hiccup and cut out. The problem lies on the broadcaster's end, and for the time being, it is something we'll all have to live with.

Bookmarking a SHOUTcast

You can save and recall SHOUTcast locations. When listening to a SHOUTcast, open up the Winamp Playlist Editor. You will notice that the location is visible in the Playlist Editor. Save that location as a playlist. Use the shortcut **Ctrl+S,** enter a name for the current SHOUTcast under File Name, and click Save. You will then be able to recall that specific SHOUTcast by opening it as a playlist and selecting the Play button on the Winamp Player. Remember to connect to the Internet before trying this.

One More SHOUT . . .

SHOUTcast is leading the way and opening the potential for true underground Internet Radio. Innovative musicians and entrepreneurs are going to take advantage of SHOUTcast's potential to spread the word. The next big push of content delivery over the Internet is likely to be Internet-only radio stations. It is too early to know exactly how the Digital Millennium Copyright Act of 1998 and earlier legislation will affect the business of Internet radio. In the meantime, exercise your right to hear the music and keep listening to the SHOUTcast of your choice.

COMING UP . . .

In Chapter 3, we'll tour a few software tools that allow you to rip and encode your CD audio tracks into MP3 files. There's something for both the Mac and Windows user. In Chapter 4, we'll take you even farther with two all-in-one ripping/encoding applications, AudioCatalyst (Mac and Windows) and MusicMatch Jukebox.

Making MP3s

3

Many scoff at the notion of people sitting in front of a computer to listen to music. . . . A couple of days ago, I was talking to a music industry exec. I told him that incoming college freshman aren't taking stereo systems into their dorm rooms anymore. They are simply attaching speakers on the now mandatory personal computer and using that as their listening station. He rolled his eyes and laughed in disbelief. He quickly sobered up when I explained that this was not 5–10 years in the future that I was talking about. This is now.

— *Michael Robertson*

IN THIS CHAPTER

- Ripping

- Encoding

- Editing the ID3 Tag

Ripping and encoding content to MP3 is more than a concept, and in this chapter and the next, it will become your reality. Initially, Chapters 3 and 4 were combined, but there is so much to say that it had to be divided between two chapters.

In this chapter, we'll go through a series of tutorials using several of the most popular ripping or encoding packages available today. With one exception, they are very inexpensive.

Warning

Current U.S. and international copyright laws forbid the unauthorized copying and distribution of music files over the Internet. Don't be the example chosen by some record company or recording artist to show the rest of the world that the law really works. Someone found guilty of posting an unauthorized song on a Web site could be fined a minimum of $500 per violation and a maximum of $20,000 per violation.

SOUND QUALITY

The overall sound quality of an MP3 file is determined by the quality of the source audio and the target resolution at which you choose to encode your file. There's also a wild card — the encoding software. If you are using a hacked-up, buggy, freeware MP3 encoder that you found replicating itself in some distant quadrant of the Internet, the sound quality of the resulting MP3 files may suffer. Free doesn't always mean good.

Tip

If such slang terms as *ripping* and *tagging* are unfamiliar to you, there is an MP3 glossary at the back of this book. If a term is missing or a new term should arise that we are all unfamiliar with, send an e-mail to webaudioguru@excite.com. The term will then be defined and posted on the update Web page at www.mp3.com/book/.

FILE RESOLUTION

A common setting for encoding MP3 music files is 128 kbps, stereo. At this resolution, you will use about 1 MB of disk space for every one minute of music. In Table 3-1, you will find an exact breakdown of the before and after of a one-minute stereo WAVE file encoded as an MP3 file at various resolutions.

Table 3-1   Audio File Comparison

File Type	File Size	File Length	File Resolution
WAVE	10.321 MB	one minute	16 bit, 44 kHz, stereo
MP3	936 KB	one minute	128 kbps, stereo
MP3	702 KB	one minute	96 kbps, stereo
MP3	468 KB	one minute	64 kbps, stereo
MP3	351 KB	one minute	32 kbps, stereo

THE TOOLS

There are a number of tools that can be used for ripping, encoding, and tagging MP3 files. Some of these are encode-only or rip-only, while others are all-in-one encoder/rippers. The all-in-one packages are covered in Chapter 4, while the rest are covered in this chapter. Table 3-2 on the next page gives you a chance to compare some of the features in a few of the most popular Windows and Macintosh applications. For the most part, Windows applications and players rule the world of MP3. The Power Mac is, however, making inroads.

Tutorial 3-1
RIPPING WITH AUDIOGRABBER

Audiograbber is well known and widely used. In fact, Xing Technologies even licensed Audiograbber to be the ripping component of their popular software AudioCatalyst for Windows (featured in Chapter 4). There are currently two versions available: the freeware version we will be using in this tutorial, and a $24.95 commercial version. The difference between the two lies in how many tracks you can rip. The freeware version of Audiograbber only allows half of the tracks of the target CD to be ripped, while the commercial version gives you to power to rip them all. While this tutorial is about ripping only, note that you can also encode to MP3 using Audiograbber (although there are some limitations). In Tutorial 3-2, we will go through the encoding process using Audiograbber.

Table 3-2   Encoding and Ripping Software

Product Name	Encoding	Ripping	OS	Version	MSRP
Audio Catalyst URL: www.xingtech.com	Yes	Yes	Win95/98	1.5	$34.95
Audio Catalyst Mac URL: www.xingtech.com	Yes	Yes	Mac	1.0	$34.95
Audiograbber (Freeware Version) URL: www.audiograbber.com-us.net/	Yes**	Yes	Win95/98/NT	1.4	freeware
Audiograbber (Commercial Version) URL: www.audiograbber.com-us.net/	Yes**	Yes	Win95/98/NT	1.4	$24.95
MusicMatch Jukebox URL: www.musicmatch.com	Yes	Yes	Win95/98	3.0	$29.95
BIAS Peak LE URL: www.bias-inc.com	Yes*	Yes	Mac	2.0	$99.95
BIAS Peak URL: www.bias-inc.com	Yes*	Yes	Mac	2.0	$499.95
Mpecker URL: www.anime.net/~go/mpeckers.html	Yes	No	Mac	1.0	freeware

 * With Macromedia Shockwave Xtra.
** Limited encoding without installing third-party freeware.

 On the Web

To complete this tutorial, you need to obtain the freeware version of Audiograbber. Point your browser to www.mp3.com/software/windows/cdrippers.html and click on the Download link for the freeware version of Audiograbber 1.4.

TOOLBOX

- Windows 95/98 or NT computer with a CD-ROM drive
- 16 MB of system RAM
- One commercially available audio CD
- Audiograbber 1.4 (freeware version)

1. Start Audiograbber, and insert an audio CD into the CD-ROM drive of your computer. Using Figure 3-1 as your reference, note that half of the ten tracks of the CD have a checkbox directly to the left of them. These are the tracks that can be enabled for ripping and encoding an audio CD track to an MP3 file in the freeware version.

 Note

Because we are dealing with the freeware version of Audiograbber, you have no control in choosing which tracks are selected to be ripped and encoded. It appears that the software makes the choice at random.

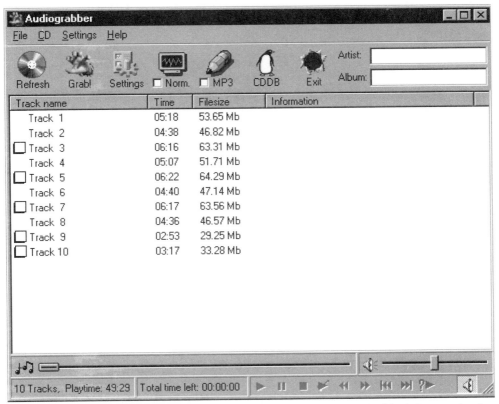

Figure 3-1   Using the freeware version of Audiograbber, half of the tracks from the target CD can be enabled for ripping and encoding. The target tracks can be identified by the checkbox directly to the left of the track name.

2. If you do not want to store your soon-to-be-ripped WAVE files in the
    Audiograbber default folder, click the Settings icon in the Audiograbber toolbar.
    In the Settings window, click the Browse button and choose a destination folder
    for your target files (see Figure 3-2). When the target folder is selected, click the
    OK button to return to the main window of Audiograbber.

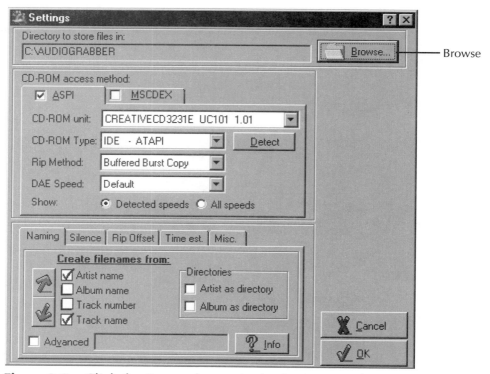

Browse

Figure 3-2   Click the Browse button in the Settings window to select a folder
for the target audio files.

 Note

Step 2 is not necessary to complete this tutorial, but you should be aware that this
option exists.

3. For the sake of simplicity and time, we are going rip just one track (although
    with the freeware version of Audiograbber you can rip any track that has a

checkbox beside it). In Figure 3-3, Track 3 has been selected as the target for ripping. Because we are working with freeware and are most likely using different CDs, the available tracks on your system may be slightly different. Just enter the track you wish to rip by selecting the checkbox directly to the left of the track.

4. Click the Grab icon (refer to Figure 3-3) in the Audiograbber toolbar. As shown in Figure 3-4, you can monitor the progress of your target audio track during the ripping process in the Copying Track window. When the selected audio track has been converted, you will be automatically returned to the main window of Audiograbber. The track that you ripped now resides as a WAVE file in the folder you selected in Step 2 of this tutorial (or in the default folder if you did not select a different one).

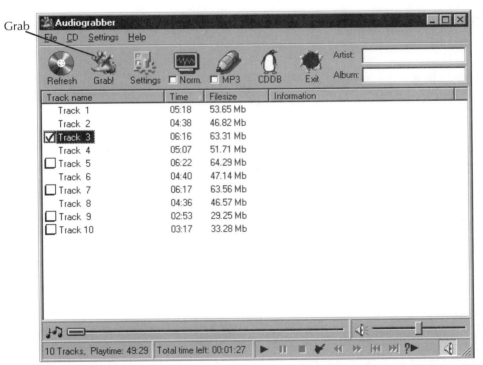

Figure 3-3   Enable the target track for ripping by enabling the checkbox directly to the left of the track.

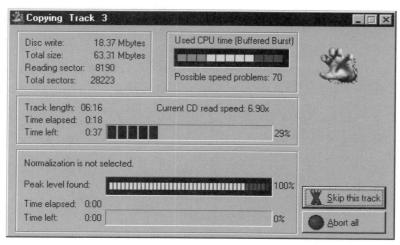

Figure 3-4   In the Copying Track window, the user can monitor the ripping process in Audiograbber. It is possible to cancel the ripping process in one or all tracks by clicking the Skip this track or Abort all buttons.

Tutorial 3-1 Retrospect

Audiograbber is the most popular ripper on the planet. There are even some low bitrate MP3 encoding features built in, potentially making Audiograbber an all-in-one ripping/encoding solution. As you can see from this last tutorial, Audiograbber makes ripping content from an audio CD a painless and almost brainless operation. Next we'll go through an easy MP3 encoding tutorial using Audiograbber and a freeware encoding application called BladeEnc.

Tutorial 3-2
ENCODING WITH AUDIOGRABBER

You may have noticed that there are limited MP3 encoding functions built into Audiograbber. There's what could best be described as a light version of the Fraunhofer MPEG 1 Level 3 (MP3) encoder that allows the user to encode files to MP3 at a maximum rate of 56 kbps (22 kHz, stereo). Since the standard of close-to-CD-quality sound in MP3 is 128 kbps (44 kHz, stereo), most users will bypass this built-in MP3 encoder. There is, however, a freeware option that can take you up to 128 kbps, and higher — BladeEnc DLL (a freeware MP3 encoder). A link to this freeware can be found at the MP3.com Web site.

On the Web

For a link to the latest release version of BladeEnc freeware encoder, go to `www.mp3.com/software/windows/encoders.html`. You must download and install BladeEnc to complete Tutorial 3-2.

Once you download and unzip the BladeEnc encoder, all you need to do is place the DLL file into the Audiograbber program directory (file folder). From there, to change the MP3 encode settings, click on the MP3 icon in the Audiograbber toolbar. This opens the MP3 Settings dialog window, where you can choose which MP3 encoder you wish to use as well as set the default encode rate. By installing the BladeEnc DLL MP3 encoder, you have turned Audiograbber into a full-fledged ripper and encoder.

TOOLBOX

- Windows 95/98 or NT computer with a CD-ROM drive
- 16 MB of system RAM
- One commercially available audio CD
- BladeEnc DLL 1.0 (or better)
- Audiograbber 1.4 (freeware version)

Let's Get Started

What you are going to do in this tutorial is to take the WAVE file that you ripped in Tutorial 3-1 and encode it to an MP3 file.

1. Start the Audiograbber and click the MP3 icon on the Audiograbber toolbar to open the MP3 Settings window (refer to Figure 3-5).

2. Because you have already downloaded and installed BladeEnc DLL, you are ready to complete Step 2. Using Figure 3-5 as your reference, Select Blade Enc DLL (version 1.00 or better) as your default MP3 encoder. From the Mode drop-down list, select a bitrate of 128 kbps and 44 Hz, stereo. Click the OK button.

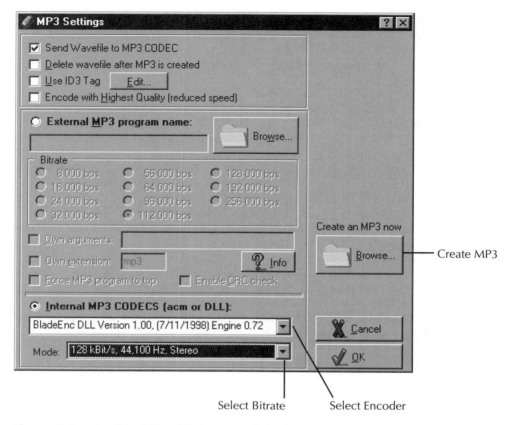

Create MP3

Select Bitrate   Select Encoder

Figure 3-5   Set BladeEnc DLL as the default MP3 encoder, and set the bitrate to 128 kBit/s, 44.100 Hz, Stereo.

3. The next step is to find the WAVE file you created in Tutorial 3-1 (or any other WAVE file). Begin in the main window of Audiograbber. Select File+Make MP3 (see Figure 3-6), and the Select File(s) window shown in Figure 3-7 opens. Choose your target WAVE file, and click Open to begin the encoding process.

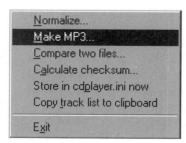

Figure 3-6   Select File+Make MP3 to open the Select File(s) window.

Figure 3-7   Select the target WAVE file for encoding, and click Open to begin the encoding process.

That's It!

Well, sort of. Using BladeEnc DLL to encode a file to MP3 is a lengthy process. The target WAVE file ripped in Tutorial 3-1 was a little over six minutes in length and will take about ten minutes to encode. Using Figure 3-8 as a reference, you can see that both Time elapsed and Time left (to encode) is displayed. Still, it is free.

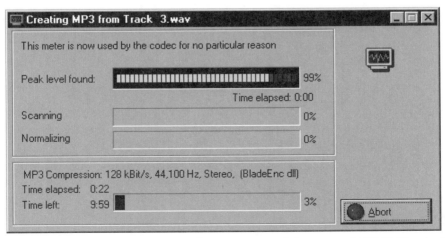

Figure 3-8   You can monitor the progress of the target WAVE file during the encoding process.

Tutorial 3-2 Retrospect

As you can see, encoding a file to MP3 with Audiograbber is a simple process. But still, there may be questions. This section will answer some of them.

First, there's another quick way to create an MP3 (refer to Figure 3-5). By clicking on Browse, you will open up the Select File(s) window. Choose a WAVE file, and click Open to begin the encoding process.

One-Step Ripping and Encoding

Here's a good question that you might already be asking yourself: How about one-step ripping and encoding with Audiograbber? No problem. Go back and redo Tutorial 3-1 starting from Step 1, but with one simple difference: On the Audiograbber toolbar, select the MP3 icon by clicking in the checkbox directly to the left of it. This combines the ripping and encoding process. Again, the most notable downside of using BladeEnc with Audiograbber is the considerable length of time to rip and encode a CD track.

Compact Disc Database (CDDB)

Here's another question that will be answered in depth in the upcoming Chapter 4: What is CDDB? It is the online Compact Disc Database. If you have a commercially available audio CD in the CD-ROM drive of your computer and Audiograbber (or any one of many ripping/encoding applications) is running, you can connect to this database on the Internet. Your application will search the huge database of commercially available CD track information, locate the CD that's in your CD-ROM drive, and assign the correct track information to each track you rip and encode. It will also save this information in the ID3 Tag of the encoded MP3 file.

Setting up the CDDB in Audiograbber is as easy as clicking on the Settings drop-down menu and selecting CDDB Settings. Click the Get List button, choose a location from the selection that pops up, enter your e-mail address in the E-mail settings, and click OK. Then, click the CDDB icon on the Audiograbber toolbar, and your computer will go online and search the database for the information on the audio CD in the computer's CD-ROM drive. CDDB is a simple yet useful function that has become a part of most of the CD rippers and encoders.

One Final Thought

With the exception of the amount of time it requires to encode a file to MP3, Audiograbber is an excellent program. The current price of Xing Technologies' AudioCatalyst is only $5 more than the full commercial version of Audiograbber, and as far as encoding goes, AudioCatalyst leaves Audiograbber in the dust. The ripping portion of Audiograbber has been licensed by Xing and is part of AudioCatalyst. Xing claims their MP3 encoder can rip eight times faster than the closest competition.

Tutorial 3-3
RIPPING WITH BIAS PEAK 2.0

In the world of music and computers, the Macintosh has been the platform of choice for professional musicians and studio engineers alike. To date, the majority of high-end computer music systems are still Mac-based. This is now changing: Digidesign recently ported Pro Tools over to Windows NT, and there are many Windows choices, including CoolEdit Pro and Sound Forge. But for many professionals, the Mac is still the platform of choice.

BIAS Peak was a latecomer to a world dominated by sound editing and recording software from Digidesign. The release of Peak 2.0 late in 1998 could not have been timed better. Those who work in the world of DAWs (Digital Audio Workstations) have been in need of an improved replacement for Digidesign's Sound Designer II, and Peak 2.0 does everything they could ask for and a lot more.

In addition to being a flexible audio editing and mastering tool, Peak 2.0 makes ripping and converting audio to the MP3 format simple. Because of the $499.95 list price of Peak 2.0, the target audience of this application is professional musicians and Mac-based recording studios. If you are serious about creating high-quality audio content and plan on posting demos of your music in MP3 (or any other format), Peak 2.0 is the ticket.

 Note

To find BIAS Peak 2.0 on the Web, go to www.bias-inc.com. The current MSRP on Peak 2.0 is $499.95, although some music retailers discount it as much as 20 percent. In addition to Peak 2.0, Peak LE 2.0, the light, less-costly version of Peak, is available for $99.95. You can complete the following tutorial using either Peak LE 2.0 or Peak 2.0.

TOOLBOX

- Any Power Macintosh computer with CD-ROM drive
- 32 MB of system RAM
- System 7.5 (or higher)
- Apple's Sound Manager 3.3 (or higher)
- A hard drive with 18 millisecond seek time (or faster)
- 13-inch (or larger) color monitor

- QuickTime 3.0 (or higher)
- QuickTime PowerPlug, installed in the Extensions folder
- Audio CD
- BIAS Peak 2.0 or Peak LE 2.0

Let's Get Started

1. Load the audio CD into the CD-ROM drive of your Power Mac and start BIAS Peak 2.0 or Peak LE 2.0.

2. From the File pull-down menu, select Import CD Track. This opens the Select Tracks To Import dialog window.

3. Select the track you wish to rip by single-clicking on it (this highlights the target track) and then clicking the Mark button shown in Figure 3-9.

4. Click the Set Import Times button to open the Audio CD Import Options window shown in Figure 3-10.

5. In the Settings area, select 44.100 kHz for the Rate, 16 bit for the Size, and Stereo for the Use (refer to Figure 3-10). Also, note that under Audio Selection, you can preview the target track by pressing Play. Even better, you can set the Start and End times of the target audio track. This function can be useful if you plan to extract portions of audio from a CD track. When you have finished entering the correct settings, click OK to continue.

6. Next, click the Import Button (refer to Figure 3-9) in the Select Tracks To Import window, and select a destination folder for the target audio as shown in Figure 3-11. Click the Save button to start the ripping process. When ripping is finished, the target audio file is opened in Peak for you to use.

Figure 3-9   Click on Track 1, and then click the Mark button.

Figure 3-10   Copy these settings as the default for your target audio files.

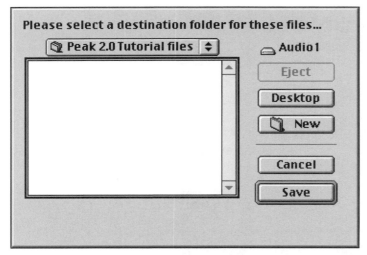

Figure 3-11   Select the destination folder for your target audio file, and click Save to begin the ripping process.

Tutorial 3-3 Retrospect

Ripping, *CD audio import*, and *digital audio extraction* are all terms for the same thing. "Ripping" is probably a less elegant term than "digital audio extraction," but it has been adopted by MP3ers as the description of choice. Both Peak 2.0 and Peak LE will flawlessly rip audio content from a CD. What gives Peak a great advantage over the less-expensive ripping-only applications is what you can do with and to the file once it is in your system. If you are a musician or recording engineer, chances are that you are creating music and sound of your own. You may wish to remix an existing track or create a compilation of your own work. Peak offers an amazing number of high-quality Digital Signal Processing (DSP) options as well as the ability to use Premiere, Audiosuite, and Pro Tools TDM audio effects plug-ins. By downloading the Macromedia Shockwave Xtra (`http://download.macromedia.com/pub/updates/SE16SWA.hqx`) and installing it in the Peak Plug-in folder, you can also use Peak to convert standard audio files into either MP3 or Shockwave audio files. As a bonus, Adaptec's Toast (CD-burning software) is bundled with Peak 2.0, and you can burn an audio CD directly from a Peak playlist. Using the Web and MP3 as the delivery system, many musicians will have, for the first time ever, a chance to put their work in front of millions of potential fans and critics.

Tutorial 3-4
ENCODING WITH MPECKER (MAC)

To say that the choices are few and far between for MP3 encoding software for the Mac is an understatement. With the release of AudioCatalyst for the Mac (see Chapter 4, Tutorial 4-2), there is finally a full-featured MP3 ripper and encoder for sale, but there are other options as well. Following is a tutorial on an easy-to-use piece of freeware called MPecker. While MPecker is currently freeware, at some point it may go out of beta and become shareware.

TOOLBOX

- Any Power Macintosh computer with CD-ROM drive
- An AIFF or SD II audio file
- Mpecker 1.0 (beta 11 or better)

 Note

To find and download the most current version of MPecker, go to
`www.anime.net/~go/mpeckers.html`.

1. Start MPecker 1.0 (shown in Figure 3-12), and select File+Preferences (from the File pull-down menu) to open the Mpecker Preferences window. Use Figure 3-13 as your guide to set the MPecker Preferences, then click the OK button.

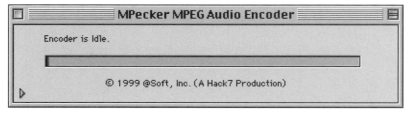

Figure 3-12   If simplicity is beauty, Mpecker wins a prize.

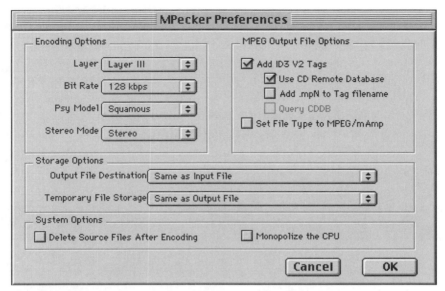

Figure 3-13   Using this figure as your template, set your MPecker Preferences to mirror those shown here, and click OK when finished.

 Note

There are a few settings in the MPecker Preferences that remain mysterious. If and when we determine how "Squamous" (seen as an Encoding Option under Psy Model) relates to MP3, and if it is significant, the answer will be posted on the Chapter 3 update page at www.mp3.com/book/.

2. The next step is to choose an appropriate audio file to encode. Select File+Open (or **Command+O**) and choose an appropriate AIFF or Sound Designer II file to encode. Select the file, and click Open to begin the encoding process. As shown in Figure 3-14, you can monitor the encoding process. To terminate the encoding process before it is finished, quit MPecker.

3. Immediately following the encode process, the MPecker ID3 Tag Editor automatically launches (see Figure 3-15). If there is relevant information (Title/Artist/Album) that you would like to embed into your MP3 file, enter it in the appropriate fields and click OK. ID3 Tag information will show up visually in many MP3 players. If you choose to leave these fields blank, click No Tags. MPecker automatically quits after a file has been encoded.

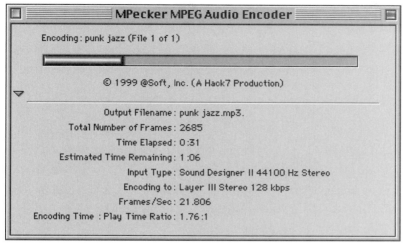

Figure 3-14   MPecker allows you to monitor the encoding process.

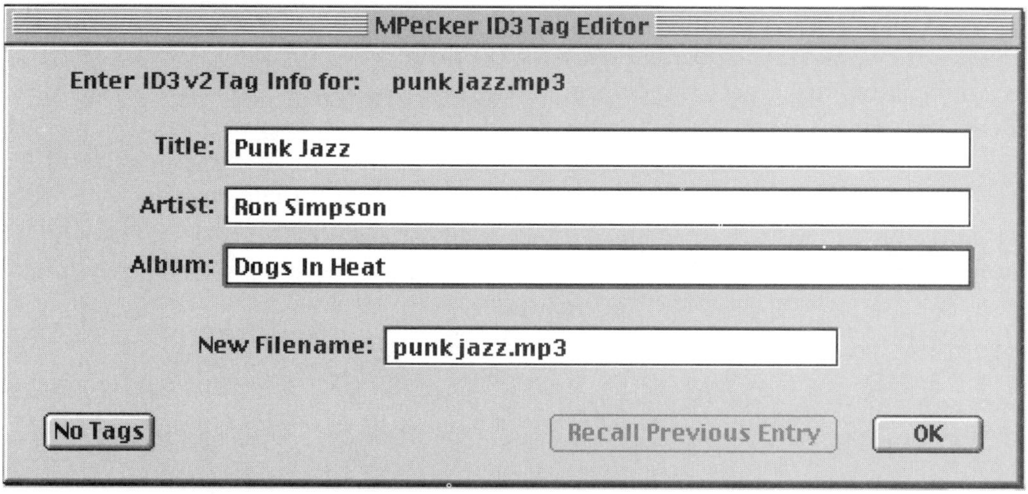

Figure 3-15   The MPecker ID3 Tag Editor automatically launches after the target file has been encoded.

Tutorial 3-4 Retrospect

First and foremost, MPecker is currently the only freeware/shareware Mac-based MP3 encoder available. Once you set the preferences, you simply choose a file and open it to begin the encoding process. It doesn't get much easier than that. At this point, you might be wondering what the story is behind the ID3 Tag that showed up in Step 3. Tutorials 3-5 and 3-6 should answer any questions you have about using and editing an ID3 Tag.

TAG EDITING

The ID3 Tag supplies information when playing back an MP3 file. An ID3 Tag is 128 bytes of information that is tagged onto the end of an MP3 file. The user is allowed to enter song title, artist, and album information that will travel as a part the MP3 file. With the informal release of ID3, version 2, some tag editors also include fields for year, genre, and comments as well as the opportunity to insert graphics, lyrics, and EQ presets. This next set of tutorials is a quick tour of how to edit and save an ID3 Tag on a Mac and a Windows computer.

Tutorial 3-5
THE MACAMP TAG EDITOR

In Step 3 of Tutorial 3-4, you might have been caught off guard when the MPecker ID3 Tag Editor popped up with no prompting whatsoever. In Mpecker, the only chance that you have to edit the ID3 Tag is right after the encoding process has been completed. If you decide to make some additional changes after the fact, you need to go to a different application. That is where the MacAmp Tag Editor (MATE) can come in handy. MATE is freeware that gives you some basic tag-editing capabilities, but that's about it. The first step is to download MATE and install it in your Mac OS 8 computer.

 Note

The MacAmp Tag Editor (MATE) can be found on the Web and downloaded for free at www.macamp.com/mate/.

TOOLBOX

- Any Power Macintosh computer running Mac OS8 (or higher)
- An MP3 file
- MacAmp 1.0 (or higher)

1. Start MATE, and from the File pull-down menu select Open (**Command+O**). Select the target MP3 file (as shown in Figure 3-16), and click Open to complete this step.

2. MATE enables the user to enter information into five separate fields. Using Figure 3-17 as your reference, enter the relevant information from your target MP3 file into each of the five fields. Under Genre, you may either enter your own description or choose from numerous preset descriptions that are accessed by clicking the button directly to the right of the Genre field.

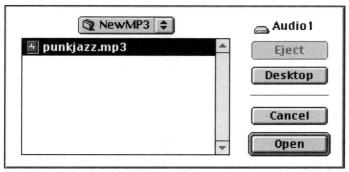

Figure 3-16   Select and open the target MP3 file to which you wish to add ID3 Tag information.

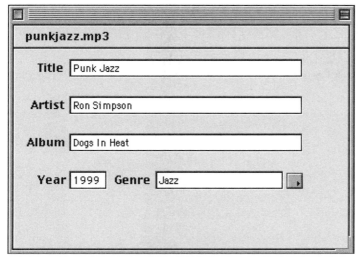

Figure 3-17   Information entered into each of the five fields will be saved as an ID3 Tag.

3. From the File pull-down menu, select Save to complete this tutorial (or use **Command+S**). The new ID3 version 2 Tag information that you created in MATE is now saved as an ID3 Tag on the target MP3 file.

Tutorial 3-5 Retrospect

There really isn't a whole lot to this early release version of MATE. You open the application, insert the info in the proper fields, and save it. Future revisions of MATE may offer fields for lyrics, cover art, and more. As MATE matures, look for feature updates at www.mp3.com/book/.

Tutorial 3-6
TAG EDITING WITH WINAMP

Winamp is the most-used MP3 player on many computers, with something like 10 million Winamp players downloaded at last count. If you haven't already downloaded and installed this shareware MP3 player, there is no time like the present to do so.

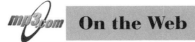 **On the Web**

Go straight to www.mp3.com/software/windows/players.html and click the Winamp link. It's a free download, but remember that it is shareware, so don't forget to register the program and pay the $10 fee.

TOOLBOX

- Winamp 2.09 or higher (installed)
- An MP3 file
- Windows 95/98

1. Start Winamp, hit **L** on your keyboard to access the Open File directory, and load an MP3 file into the Winamp Player (refer to Figure 3-18). Any MP3 file will do.

2. Select **Alt+3** to open the MPEG File Info Box + ID3 Tag Editor dialog box. If there is no ID3 Tag information saved in your test MP3 file, all fields (with the exception of Title) will be empty (refer to Figure 3-19). If you wish to clear all information from an ID3 Tag, click the Remove ID3 button.

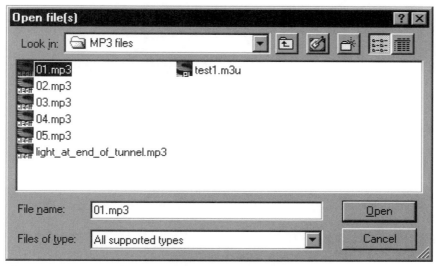

Figure 3-18 Load an MP3 file into the Winamp Player.

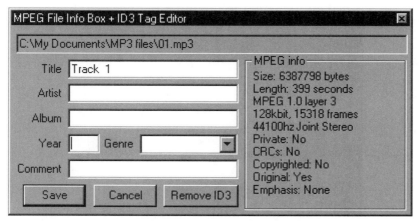

Figure 3-19 To clear all information except Title from the ID3 Tag Editor, click the Remove ID3 button.

3. Using Figure 3-20 for reference, enter the relevant information in each of the appropriate fields. Note that to choose a Genre (field 5), you must click the

button directly to the right of the Genre field and select from one of the many presets that are provided. When finished, click Save.

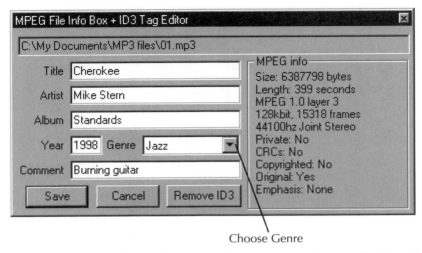

Figure 3-20   Click the button to the right of the Genre field to choose from one of the many Genre presets.

Tutorial 3-6 Retrospect

Once you know what an ID3 Tag is, there really isn't a whole lot to writing or editing one and saving it as part of an MP3 file. In Step 2, depending on the MP3 file you choose to use, there may already be ID3 Tag information that is saved with the file. By clicking the Remove ID3 button, you will be able to start with a clean slate, or you can simply overwrite each of the fields one at a time.

The Mercedes of Tag Editors

MusicMatch Jukebox 3.0 (MMJB 3.0) has shown up in each of the first three chapters for good reason; it is a product with depth. The Tag Editor in MMJB offers almost too many information fields. As you can see in Figure 3-21, not only are the basic fields (Artist, Album, and so forth) covered, but there are user fields for Lyrics, Artist e-mail, and a whole lot more. From an e-commerce stand-point, being able to enter a Buy CD URL into the ID3 Tag is a stroke of marketing genius. If a listener were to download and really like a free promotional MP3 track, the chances are pretty good that the potential customer just might click on the Buy CD URL and do just that.

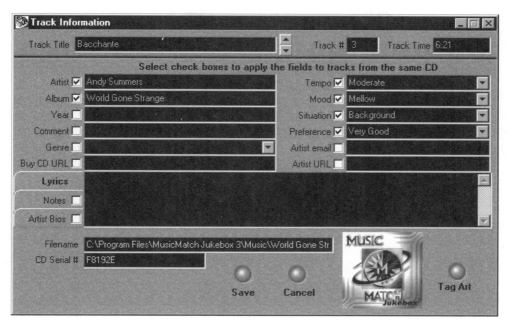

Figure 3-21   The Tag Editor in MusicMatch Jukebox 3.0 is about as full-featured as you can find and even includes an option for album cover Tag Art.

Accessing the Tag Editor on MMJB 3.0 is as easy as opening the Music Library and clicking the Tag button. After entering or editing data into the Track Information window, all that is needed is a click of the OK button to save the data. Interestingly enough, data saved into an MP3 file using the MMJB Tag Editor doesn't show up on the Winamp Player. In short, that would mean the information that resides in the MMJB 3.0 ID Tag is proprietary in nature. However, in the very near future, users of MusicMatch Jukebox will be able to tag their MP3 files with either an ID3 Tag or MMJB Tag. Chances are that this feature will be added before you read this book.

CHAPTER RETROSPECT

This chapter has introduced ripping and encoding. Chapter 4 covers tutorials and tours of all-in-one ripping and encoding software from Xing Technologies (AudioCatalyst for both Windows and Mac) as well as Brava Software's MusicMatch Jukebox 3.0.

On the Web

Like phone numbers and e-mail addresses, links can change. Your best bet while working with this or any other chapter in this book is to go directly to `www.mp3.com/book/`. From there, link to the relevant chapter update page, and you will have access to the latest information about featured software and technology and current links.

4

All-in-One Tutorials: Ripping and Encoding

The biggest danger to artists is not being heard, which is a surefire recipe for failure. Only through exposure does music get appreciated and subsequently CDs sold, concerts attended, fan bases established, etc.

—*Michael Robertson*

IN THIS CHAPTER

- AudioCatalyst 1.5 for Windows

- AudioCatalyst 1.0 for Macintosh

- MusicMatch Jukebox 3.0

There are a couple of all-in-one products that make ripping and encoding audio from a CD to MP3 files a quick and easy one-step process. Sort of like a smart weapon: Fire it and forget it. AudioCatalyst from Xing Technologies and MusicMatch Jukebox from Brava Software fit this category perfectly. If you have yet to purchase either of these applications, use these tutorials to see how they work.

If you run into terms that are unfamiliar to you, check the Glossary at the end of this book.

Tip

The Compact Disc Database (CDDB) is a cool Web resource that could save you lots of time. It is an online database that catalogs the album, artist, and title information of just about every audio CD produced. Each of the applications featured in this chapter can automatically access the online CDDB. What that means is that when you pop a commercially available audio CD into your CD-ROM drive and use this feature, the program will locate the CDDB and will automatically tag your MP3 file with the basic info you want and need by creating an ID3 Tag (which is basically an identification tag for each tune). You can go back and edit the ID3 Tag at a later date. For more information on CDDB, visit their Web site at www.cddb.com.

Tutorial 4-1
AUDIOCATALYST 1.5 FOR WINDOWS

AudioCatalyst (Xing Technologies) is an easy-to-use, reasonably priced solution for ripping and encoding. This application combines the Xing MP3 Encoder (audio only) and Audiograbber ripping software into one package. This tutorial will guide you through the setup process. Once you have set the parameters, preferences, and the destination for your soon-to-be-converted MP3 files, the ripping and encoding process are simple.

On the Web

If you don't have it yet, download the trial version of AudioCatalyst from the MP3.com Web site: www.mp3.com/software/windows/encoders.html.

Note

At the end of this (and every) tutorial is a retrospect to further explain the different possibilities that are available.

TOOLBOX

- Pentium 166 processor
  with 16 MB of RAM
  (32 MB recommended)
- Windows 95/98 or NT 4.0
- Audio sound card
- CD-ROM drive that supports
  digital extraction (ripping)

- AudioCatalyst 1.5
- One commercially available
  audio CD

Let's Get Started

1. Create a new folder as the destination for your soon-to-be ripped and encoded MP3 file and name it **MP3TEST1**.
2. Insert the target audio CD into the CD-ROM drive of your computer.
3. Launch AudioCatalyst 1.5. The main screen is shown in Figure 4-1.

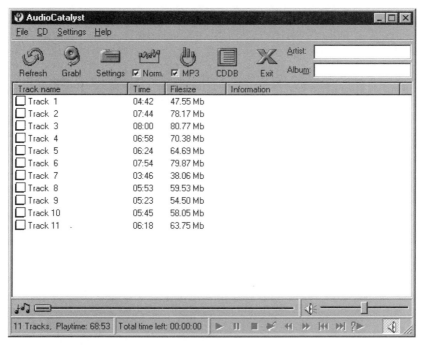

Figure 4-1   The main window of AudioCatalyst 1.5 lists the tracks it finds on the audio CD, along with their length and size.

4. To set the destination folder for your encoded MP3 file, click the Settings button (refer to Figure 4-1) on the AudioCatalyst toolbar.

   In the resulting Settings window, click the Browse button (see Figure 4-2), and in the Select Directory dialog box that opens (refer to Figure 4-3), choose the target folder (in this case, **MP3TEST1**). Click OK to exit the Select Directory, and once again click OK to exit the Settings directory.

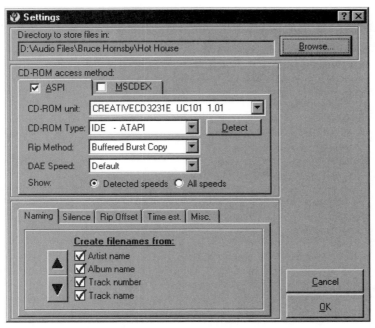

Figure 4-2   Click the Browse button in the Settings window to open the Select Directory dialog box.

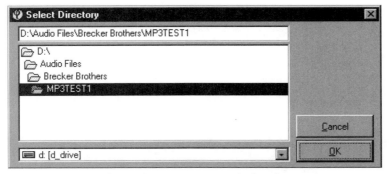

Figure 4-3   In the Select Directory dialog box, choose a target folder (**MP3TEST1** in this case) as the location for encoded MP3 files.

5. The next step is to set the Encoder Settings. Click the MP3 button on the AudioCatalyst toolbar (refer to Figure 4-1) to open the XingMP3 Encoder Settings window. For the sake of simplicity, duplicate the settings that are shown in Figure 4-4. When finished, click the OK button to return to the main page of AudioCatalyst.

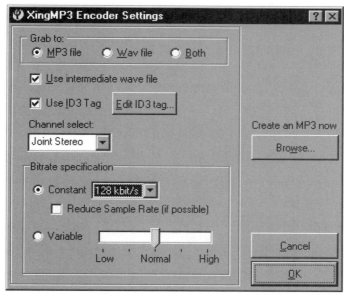

Figure 4-4   Duplicate these Encoder Settings.

6. The next step is to enter the Artist and Album names and select the individual track you wish to rip and encode. On the far right side of the AudioCatalyst toolbar are two fields in which you can enter the names of an artist and album (refer to Figure 4-5). It is important to enter this information before the ripping and encoding begins, as this is the source for the ID3 Tag.

7. Under Track name, choose the track number you are going to rip and encode. In this case, select Track 1.

8. Make sure that Norm (Normalization) and MP3 are checked (see the checkmarks in the corresponding boxes just under these toolbar buttons in Figure 4-5).

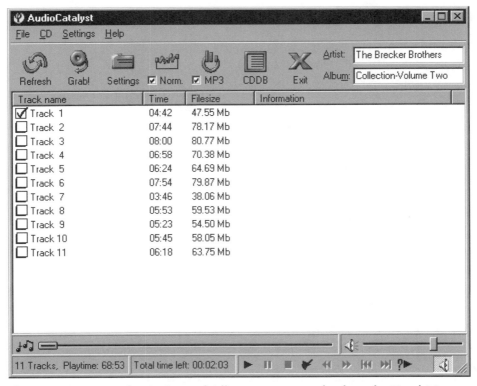

Figure 4-5   Enter the Artist and Album names and select the Track(s) you wish to rip and encode.

9. This is the final step. From the AudioCatalyst toolbar, click the Grab button. This starts the ripping and encoding process. Be patient, as it takes two or more minutes per track to complete the process. When Copied OK appears in the Information column of the main screen (see Figure 4-6), the ripping and encoding process is successfully completed.

Track name	Time	Filesize	Information
☑ Track 1	04:42	47.55 Mb	Copied OK, Checksum: 5014FB33

Figure 4-6   The ripping and encoding process is successfully completed when Copied OK appears under the Information heading.

Warning

It is against U.S. and international copyright law to distribute and/or sell music or any copyright-protected intellectual property without the written permission of the copyright holder. This includes posting MP3 files of copyrighted music on the Internet or making copies. Buying a music CD does not mean that you own the content. You merely have permission (also known as a *license*) from the legal owners of the material on that CD to listen to it in a noncommercial setting.

Tutorial 4-1 Retrospect

As you can see, once you have AudioCatalyst set up properly, it is an easy application to use. Looking back to the tutorial, you probably have a few questions about some of the steps.

ID3 Tag (Step 5)

There are a number of optional settings that allow you to control the file size and sound quality of the MP3 track you are about to encode. Referring back to Figure 4-4, you will notice that the Use ID3 Tag is checkmarked. Now you're about to find out why. Go back to step 5 of the tutorial, and click the MP3 icon on the toolbar to open up the Encoder Settings window. Select the Edit ID3 tag button, and click it once with your left mouse button. As you can see in Figure 4-7, this opens the ID3 Tag Editor. This is where you enter the song's name and alter or add any other relevant information. When you have finished entering or editing the content, click the OK button to close the ID3 Tag Editor window.

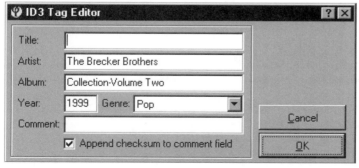

Figure 4-7   The ID3 Tag Editor window of AudioCatalyst is where you enter vital information about the tunes.

Bitrate Specification (Step 5)

Refer again to Figure 4-4, specifically to the Bitrate specification area of the window. Notice that Constant and a bitrate of 128 kbit/s are checked. Most people believe that if you encode music at a bitrate of less than 128 kbit/s, the results will be less than pleasant to listen to. At 128 kbit/s, stereo, your file size is going to be about 1 MB of disk space per minute. The setting of 128 kbit/s is considered the standard for high-quality music playback of an MP3 file.

The other option in the Bitrate specification area is called Variable. While this is a cool function, playback of an MP3 file that has been encoded using the Variable process is not always acceptable. Depending on the MP3 player you are using, there may be glitches and hiccups. If you enable Variable bitrate, it allows AudioCatalyst to change the bitrate during the encoding process when certain situations are met. For example, when there is a spot in the song where there is no sound, the encoder switches to the lowest bitrate possible. This can save a considerable amount of disk space, depending on the CD audio or WAVE file you happen to be encoding. On the other hand, when there is music, sound, or spoken word coming through, the Xing encoder uses the highest bitrate possible according to where you set the slider. As time goes by, you will probably see a number of encoders adopting the Variable bitrate settings.

Norm and MP3 Checkboxes (Step 8)

In step 8, you selected the Norm and MP3 checkboxes. By selecting the Norm (Normalize) button, you are applying a process to the target audio track(s) that amplifies the volume of the target audio to the maximum level it can achieve without causing distortion. If you want the target audio that you are ripping to be encoded to MP3, it is necessary to select the MP3 checkbox on the AudioCatalyst Toolbar.

Quickie Tutorial:
Using the Compact Disc Database (CDDB)

On the AudioCatalyst toolbar, note the button called CDDB. This is an abbreviation for Compact Disc Database, an online database that catalogs just about every commercially available audio CD ever released. In this quickie tutorial, we'll show you how to set the CDDB preferences and make it work within AudioCatalyst 1.5. Make sure AudioCatalyst is up and running. The computer you are using must be able to connect to the Internet as you will be going online during the tutorial.

1. Before you begin to use the CDDB, you have to configure it to work
    properly. Directly above the AudioCatalyst toolbar are four drop-down
    menus (refer to Figure 4-1). From the Settings menu, select CDDB
    Settings to open the CDDB Settings window (see Figure 4-8).

 Note

Don't confuse the Settings pull-down menu with the Settings toolbar button. While
you can access the General Settings from the Settings button, the reverse is not true.
Similarly, don't be hasty and click on the CDDB toolbar button before you configure
the settings. That button is used to access the CDDB, not adjust its settings.

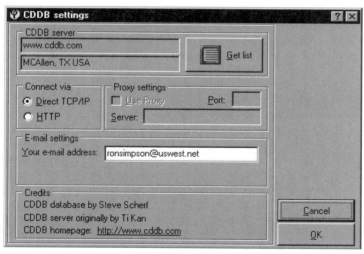

Figure 4-8   The CDDB Settings window is where you configure the software to
find the online CD database.

2. Under E-mail settings, enter your e-mail address, and click the OK
    button to exit the CDDB Settings window.

3. On the AudioCatalyst toolbar, click the CDDB button. Once the
    connection is made, the database will recognize the CD that is in your
    CD-ROM drive and automatically enter the artist, album, and the track
    name of each individual song. Figure 4-9 shows some sample results. By
    using the CDDB before you rip and encode a music CD, this informa-
    tion will become part of the ID3 tag, saving you lots of
    time and frustration.

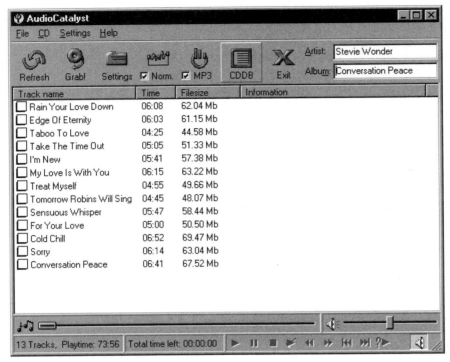

Figure 4-9   The CDDB will recognize the audio CD in your CD-ROM drive and automatically enter the artist, album, and track names.

Toolbar Tour

Figure 4-10 and Table 4-1 provide a basic explanation of each of the items in the AudioCatalyst toolbar.

Figure 4-10   The AudioCatalyst toolbar gives you quick access to the seven common functions of the software.

Table 4-1   The AudioCatalyst Toolbar

Tool Button	Explanation
Refresh	Click this icon to refresh the information in the track list.
Grab	Click this icon to begin the ripping and encoding process.
Settings	Click this icon to access the general settings of AudioCatalyst.
Norm.	Click this icon to adjust the normalization settings of AudioCatalyst.*
MP3	Click this icon to set the encoder settings for the target MP3 files.*
CDDB	Click this icon to access the online CD database.
Exit	Click this icon to exit AudioCatalyst.

* If you wish to normalize and / or encode a file to MP3, be sure to that the Norm and MP3 checkboxes are checked.

Ripping or Encoding

At some point, you may wish to encode an already existing WAVE file or create a separate WAVE file from an audio CD with no intent of encoding it to an MP3. With AudioCatalyst, you are able to do both.

Quickie Tutorial: Ripping Only

If any part of this mini tutorial is confusing, refer back to Tutorial 4-1.

1. Fire up AudioCatalyst 1.5.

2. Insert the target audio CD in the CD-ROM drive of your computer.

3. Set a destination folder for the target WAVE file. If you are unfamiliar with this process, refer back to step 4 in Tutorial 4-1 for the specifics.

4. Because you do not want the WAVE file that you are about to extract from the audio CD to be encoded to MP3, deselect the MP3 checkbox on the AudioCatalyst Toolbar.

5. From the Track name list, select the CD audio track to be ripped.

6. From the AudioCatalyst toolbar, click on the Grab button. Providing you followed all of the previous steps correctly, AudioCatalyst is now extracting the CD audio track and converting it to a WAVE file.

Quickie Tutorial: Encode Only

This one is really easy. Let's use the premise that you have an existing WAVE file that you wish to encode to MP3.

1.   Launch AudioCatalyst 1.5.

2.   On the AudioCatalyst toolbar, click the MP3 button.

3.   You are now in the Encoder Settings window. Click the Browse button, and select the WAVE file you wish to encode.

4.   Click the Open button, and the MP3 encoding process will begin.

Quickie Tutorial Retrospect

If you completed or at least read Tutorial 4-1, the fine points left out of these two quickie tutorials will not have escaped you. There are certain situations in which the singular process of ripping or encoding will be needed, and it's nice to know that AudioCatalyst gives the user that option.

Final Thoughts on AudioCatalyst

AudioCatalyst is powerful, well thought out, easy to use, and most importantly for many of us, reasonably priced. If we were reviewing AudioCatalyst for a magazine article, we would give it a five-star rating.

Tutorial 4-2
AUDIOCATALYST 1.0 FOR THE MAC

With the impending release of AudioCatalyst 1.0 for the Mac, Xing provided a pre-release beta version, which we reviewed for this chapter. While there were a few small bugs in the beta, all aspects of this application are up and running. You will notice as you view the main screen of the Mac version of AudioCatalyst 1.0 (refer to Figure 4-11) that it looks nothing like its more mature Windows counterpart. This, however, is no problem: AudioCatalyst 1.0 works like a charm and gives you access to all the functions needed to rip and encode to MP3.

Note

To complete Tutorial 4-2, you need AudioCatalyst 1.0 (or better) for the Macintosh. For information on how to purchase AudioCatalyst for the Macintosh, go to the Xing Technology home page at `www.xingtech.com/products/audiocatalyst/`. A trial version may be available by the time you read this note.

TOOLBOX

- Power Macintosh computer with 32 MB of RAM
- System 7.5 (or better)
- CD-ROM drive
- AudioCatalyst 1.0
- One commercially available audio CD

Let's Get Started

1. Create a new folder as the destination for your soon-to-be ripped and encoded MP3 file and name it **MyMP3**.

2. Insert the target audio CD into the CD-ROM drive of your computer.

3. Launch AudioCatalyst 1.0. The main screen is shown in Figure 4-11.

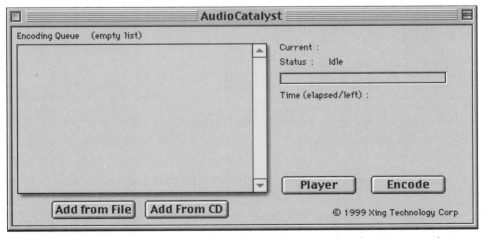

Figure 4-11 The main screen of AudioCatalyst 1.0 for the Macintosh is different than its Windows counterpart, but it works just as well.

4. In this next step, you need to set the preferences for ripping and encoding your target audio. From the pull-down menu, select File+Preferences to open up the Preferences window (shown in Figure 4-12).

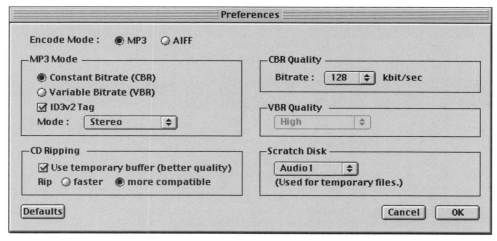

Figure 4-12   Use these preferences settings for Tutorial 4-2.

5. Using the settings shown in Figure 4-12 as your guide, make the following selections in this window:

    •   For Encode Mode, select MP3.

    •   In the MP3 Mode area, select Constant Bitrate (CBR), check ID3v2 Tag, and select the Stereo mode.

    •   In the CD Ripping area, select Use temporary buffer and enable more compatible for Rip.

    •   In the CBR Quality area, select a Bitrate of 128 kbit/sec.

    •   Under Scratch Disk, choose a hard drive as a temporary location for your audio files.

    •   Double-check to make sure the settings in your Preferences window match those shown in Figure 4-12 and click the OK button to return to the main window.

6. In this step, you are going to choose a track from the audio CD in your CD-ROM drive to encode. Click on the Add From CD button (refer back to Figure 4-11), which opens the CD Tracks window shown Figure 4-13. Select the track

you wish to rip and encode by clicking on it. Then click the Add Selected button and you will be returned to the main window.

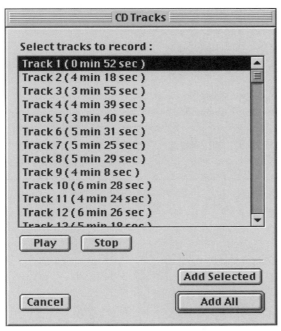

Figure 4-13   Select the track you are going to rip and encode by clicking on it in the CD Tracks window.

7. Now that you are back in the main window of AudioCatalyst, select the track you are going to rip and encode from the Encoding Queue by clicking on it (refer to Figure 4-14). Next, click the Encode button at the bottom right corner of the window. You will be asked to select a target folder for your file. Select **MyMP3**, the target file folder you created in step 1 (shown in Figure 4-15), and click the **Select "MyMP3"** button to start the ripping and encoding process.

 Note

While you are in the CD Tracks window, it is possible to play the selected track or tracks by clicking the Play button. This can be helpful when you are not sure of the program material on the individual tracks of the target CD.

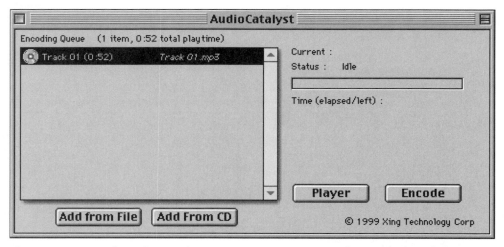

Figure 4-14   Select the track you are going to rip and encode by clicking on it and then clicking the Encode button.

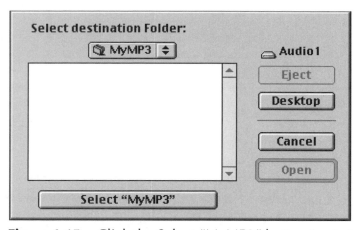

Figure 4-15   Click the Select "MyMP3" button to start ripping and encoding.

Tutorial 4-2 Retrospect

In a very short time (Xing Technology claims to have the fastest MP3 encoder on the planet), your file is ripped, encoded, and ready to be played as an MP3. As with many Macintosh applications, AudioCatalyst is very easy and intuitive to use. Although there are not nearly as many options as are available with the Windows version of the software, it delivers the goods as advertised. The bottom line with AudioCatalyst for the Mac is that it is an easy-to-use, high-quality ripping and encoding solution that doesn't cost an arm and a leg.

Setting Preferences (Step 5)

The reason for choosing Constant Bitrate in step 5 is that some MP3 players sort of freak out (or don't work at all) and hiccup when trying to play a variable bitrate MP3 file. The unofficial standard for almost-CD-quality in an MP3 file is 128 kbit/sec stereo. Anything less is not all that pleasant to listen to.

Adding More Tracks (Step 6)

Referring back to step 6, if you plan on ripping and encoding all of the tracks on the target audio CD, click the Add All button. This moves all of the tracks from the CD into the Encoding Queue. Before you rip and encode an entire CD, look ahead to the CDDB quickie tutorial on the next page. You'll be glad you did.

Ripping or Encoding with AudioCatalyst (Mac)

Ripping only with AudioCatalyst for the Mac is possible, although you have no control over the attributes of the file you are converting. Go to the Preferences window and select AIFF (instead of MP3) in the Encode Mode. Then after clicking OK, follow steps 6 and 7 from Tutorial 4-2, and the file you rip will be converted into a 16 bit 44 kHz stereo AIFF file. While you cannot set the conversion attributes, an AIFF file 16 bit 44 kHz stereo is considered a CD-quality file in the world of professional audio.

Encoding an existing audio file to an MP3 file with AudioCatalyst is as easy as clicking a couple of buttons. Refer to Tutorial 4-2, step 6, but instead of clicking on the Add From CD button, click the Add From File button. After locating the target audio file (AIFF or WAVE), click Open to add the file to the AudioCatalyst Encoding Queue. When you are ready to encode the target audio files, click the Encode button, and after a short wait, the files will be encoded.

Quickie Tutorial:
Using the Compact Disc Database (CDDB)

On the AudioCatalyst (Mac) menu bar, note the pull-down menu CDDB. This is an abbreviation for the online Compact Disc Database, a handy function can save you time and effort by recognizing the information on whatever music CD is in your CD-ROM drive and automatically entering this information in the ID3 Tag for you. Begin by going back to Tutorial 4-2 and completing the first three steps. AudioCatalyst is now up and running, a music CD is in the CD-ROM drive, and a target folder has been selected. Now you are ready for this quickie tutorial.

Note

For this quickie tutorial to work, you need to be connected to the Internet, and the target CD in your CD-ROM drive must be commercially available to be listed on the CDDB.

1. From the CDDB pull-down menu, select Set up CDDB. There are three text fields (see Figure 4-16). The first is CDDB Server. While the correct information for this text field is automatically entered as the default during the install process, it never hurts to double-check. The CDDB Server location should read `cddb.cddb.com`. In the next text field, Your e-mail address, enter your e-mail address. The third text field, Port, is too complicated to explain and beyond the scope of this book. The default for your system is correct, so there's never any need to change this. When you're finished, click the OK button. You are now set up and ready to retrieve the track, title, and artist information for the target CD.

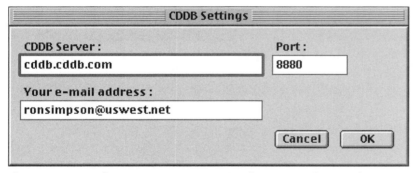

Figure 4-16   The CDDB Settings window in AudioCatalyst (Mac) is where you configure the software to find the online CD database.

2. On the main page of AudioCatalyst, click the Add From CD button. This opens the CD Tracks window (refer back to Figure 4-13). Now click the Add All button. As shown in Figure 4-17, all the tracks from the target CD will show up in the Encoding Queue of AudioCatalyst.

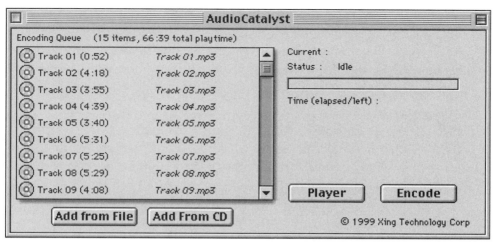

Figure 4-17   By selecting the Add All button in the CD Tracks window, all audio tracks from the target CD are shown in the Encoding Queue list.

3. From the CDDB pull-down menu, select Fetch Track Information (or **Command+T**). Your computer will briefly go online and retrieve the track information for the target CD. You can see in the Encoding Queue (shown in Figure 4-18) that each of the relevant tracks now has its proper name attached. This information also becomes part of the ID3 Tag when you encode the target tracks to MP3.

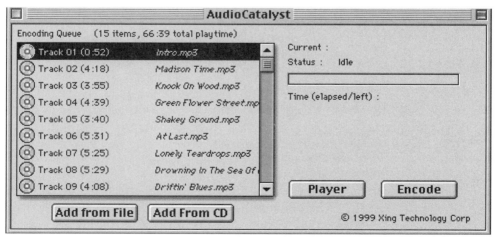

Figure 4-18   By using the CDDB feature in AudioCatalyst, each of the CD audio tracks is automatically tagged with the correct song title, artist, and album name.

4. It is possible to view and even edit track information before encoding your files to MP3. From the AudioCatalyst main window, select a track and double-click on it to open the Information window, as shown in Figure 4-19. At this point, you can edit the information that will be encoded with your MP3 file. Click the OK button when you're finished editing.

5. This last step is optional for this tutorial. Select the track or tracks you wish to encode by clicking on them in the AudioCatalyst Encoding Queue. Click the Encode button in the bottom right corner of the main window. You are then asked to select a target folder for your file. Select the target file folder (refer back to Figure 4-15), and click the Select "MyMP3" button to start the ripping and encoding process. All of the selected files will be encoded as MP3 files.

Figure 4-19   Enter or edit the ID3 tags in the Information window.

CDDB Quickie Tutorial Retrospect

The purpose of this quickie tutorial was to give you a look at how useful the CDDB function can be during the ripping and encoding process. Because you were already there (and it was relevant to the tutorial), you also learned how to edit the Track Information (also known as editing the ID3 Tag). Last but not least, because you were already all set up with a CD ready to go, it didn't hurt for you to rip and encode the entire CD. Now you know how to do just about everything there is to do with AudioCatalyst for Mac.

Tip

Setting up the default MP3 player for AudioCatalyst (Mac) is easy and necessary. From the Player pull-down menu in AudioCatalyst, choose Set Player. Locate and select the MP3 player of your choice, and click the Open button. Henceforth, when you click the Player button in the main window of AudioCatalyst, your default MP3 player will launch.

AudioCatalyst Buttons and Shortcuts

If you are new to AudioCatalyst, a basic explanation of each of the functions in the main window might be helpful. Refer to Figure 4-11 or to Table 4-2. Those of you familiar with the Windows version of AudioCatalyst will notice that you have a lot fewer choices in the Mac version.

Table 4-2   AudioCatalyst (Mac) Button and Command Functions

Button or Function	Explanation	Shortcuts
Add From File (Button)	Add an audio file to encode.	Command+O
Add From CD (Button)	Add a file from the target CD.	Command+D
Player (Button)	Launch the default MP3 player.	Command+P
Encode (Button)	Start the encoding process.	Command+R
Track Information*	Access and edit ID3 information.	Command+I
Fetch Track Information*	Accesses the CDDB.	Command+T

* Track Information and Fetch Track Information are found in the Edit and CDDB pull-down menus respectively.

And the Verdict Is . . .

Xing Technologies has another winner on their hands with AudioCatalyst for the Macintosh. The retail price is reasonable, and everything you need to successfully rip and encode to MP3 is there. As time goes on, more refinements will be added, but until then there are no real complaints.

Note

For the latest information on AudioCatalyst for the Macintosh as well as other Xing Technology products, go to www.xingtech.com.

 Tutorial 4-3
MUSICMATCH JUKEBOX 3.0 (WINDOWS)

Another Windows all-in-one package that will give you everything you need for ripping, encoding, and playback — plus a whole lot more — is MusicMatch Jukebox 3.0. One of the features hard-core MP3ers are going to love is that MusicMatch Jukebox 3.0 (MMJB 3.0) doubles as an interface to everybody's favorite MP3 portable, the Rio.

 On the Web

To complete the following tutorial you will need to use the full version of MusicMatch Jukebox 3.0 (MMJB 3.0). You can download a free feature-disabled evaluation version of the software from the MP3.com Web site at www.mp3.com/software/windows/encoders.html. If you like MusicMatch Jukebox 3.0 and wish to buy a key to unlock all of the features, the key can be purchased at the MusicMatch Web site (www.musicmatch.com). At this writing, the price of MMJB 3.0 was around $30 and includes a lifetime of free upgrades.

TOOLBOX

- Pentium 166 (or higher)
- 16 MB of RAM
- Windows 95/98
- CD-ROM player
- Sound card
- Connection to the Internet

- MusicMatch Jukebox 3.0 (full version)
- One commercially available audio CD

Let's Get Started

1. Insert the target audio CD in the CD-ROM drive of your computer, and launch MMJB 3.0. Your destination is the Jukebox area of MMJB 3.0 (use Figure 4-20 as your reference).

Figure 4-20   The Jukebox area of MusicMatch Jukebox 3.0 consists of the Player and Playlist Editor.

2. From the Options drop-down menu, select Options+View+Show Recorder. This action brings the Recorder to the front and loads the tracks from the target audio CD into the Select Tracks to Record panel, as shown in Figure 4-21.

Figure 4-21   The Recorder area of MusicMatch Jukebox 3.0 is where you load the tracks you wish to record.

3. The next step is to connect to the CDDB. Before this can happen, you need to set the CDDB preferences. Click the Options button in the MMJB Recorder window to open the Record Options window. Click the CDDB Preferences button at the bottom center of the record Options window. You are greeted by a dialog box (see Figure 4-22) that explains how to set up your CDDB preferences. Read the directions, click OK to enter the CDDB Preferences window, and set the CDDB preferences using Figure 4-23 for reference.

This next part is really a little strange. It would make sense to click the OK button, right? Not this time. After setting your preferences, click Cancel in the CDDB Preferences window, and click OK to exit the Record Options window. We're sure that having to use Cancel instead of OK is a bug that got past the programmers, but it works if you follow these directions.

 On the Web

Be sure to check the Chapter 4 update page at www.mp3.com/book/, to be advised of the fix as soon it is available.

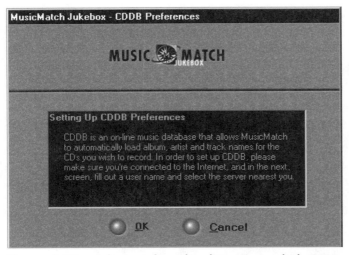

Figure 4-22   After reading the directions, click OK to enter the CDDB Preferences window.

4. Click on the CDDB button in the Recorder window (refer back to Figure 4-21) to open the CDDB Connect dialog box. After reading the instructions, click Yes to go online and retrieve the album, artist, and track information. After the connection is established, the information will be download into the Select Tracks to Record panel in the Recorder.

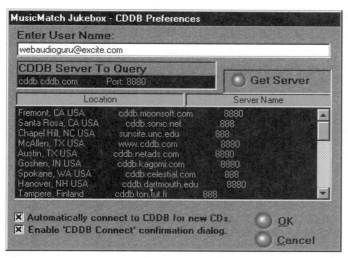

Figure 4-23   Enter your User Name and choose a CDDB Server Location.

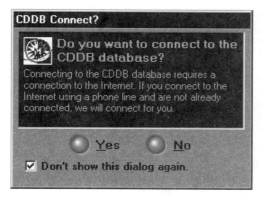

Figure 4-24   Read the connect instructions and click Yes to download the album, artist, and track information to the Recorder.

5. Before you begin ripping and encoding a file, you need to set the Record Options. In the Recorder window, click the Options button. In the Record Options dialog box, locate the Directory For New Songs (see Figure 4-25), and select the target folder in which your encoded MP3 files are going to reside. In this case, select the folder Music as shown in Figure 4-25. *Don't click the OK button just yet!!*

6. Next, you need to set the Compression Mode (also found in the Record Options window). In this case, in the CD Quality field, choose MP3 (128 kbps) (refer to Figure 4-25). In the Recording Mode field, select Digital. Once you have set the proper Record Options, click the OK button to return to the Recorder window.

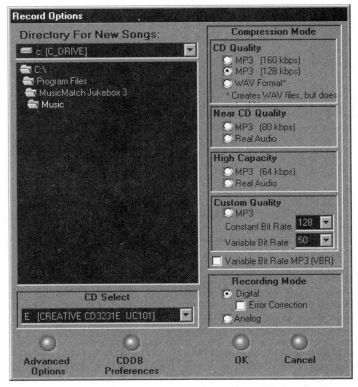

Figure 4-25   Select Music as the target folder for your soon-to-be encoded MP3 files.

7. For the sake of simplicity, we are going to rip and encode just one track in this tutorial. Select the first track by clicking the checkbox directly to the left of the target track, as shown in Figure 4-26. To begin the ripping and encoding process, click the Start button in the Recorder area. Note that your progress can be monitored during the ripping and encoding process in the Recording Status panel as well as in the Select Tracks to Record panel.

8. To hear the results, return to the Jukebox area (refer back to Figure 4-20) and select Options+View+Show Music Library. Your recently encoded MP3 file is

now sitting in the MMJB Music Library window (as shown in Figure 4-27) ready for use. There are a couple of different ways to accomplish playback. Normally, you would transfer files from the Music Library to the Playlist and play them from there. But the simplest method is to select a track (click on it) in the Music Library window. The Track Indicator Arrow will pop up directly to the left of the track that you have selected. Click on the Track Indicator Arrow and the track will begin to play in the Jukebox area, entirely bypassing the Playlist. This handy function can be used to preview a track before dragging it into the Playlist.

Figure 4-26 Select the first track by clicking the checkbox directly to the left of the target track, and click the Start button in the Recorder window to begin ripping and encoding the target track.

Figure 4-27 Click the target MP3 track and then the Track Indicator Arrow directly to the left of the track to initiate playback from the Music Library.

Tutorial 4-3 Retrospect

Upon starting MMJB 3.0, someone new to the world of MP3 or computers would have absolutely no idea how to enable the ripping and encoding functions. While the learning curve may be higher than it is with AudioCatalyst, the built-in Music Library Database is a logical way to keep track and organize MP3 files.

Organizing Your Music (Step 5)

Upon installation of MusicMatch Jukebox 3.0, a folder called Music is automatically created as the default for your MP3 files. Of course, you are free to create a folder (or series of folders) in which to store your MP3 files. Most people have their own preferences as to how to organize their home CD collection (by category, artist, or alphabetical listing, for example).

Compression Mode Settings (Step 6)

For the CD Quality setting, 128 kbps seems to be the de facto standard for near-CD-quality encoding. If you go any lower than 128 kbps, the degradation in sound quality becomes blatantly obvious when listening to music. In a nutshell, the lower you go in kbps, the worse it sounds.

Another potentially useful feature is the Custom Quality field (refer back to Figure 4-25). Variable Bitrate does have an advantage if disk space is at a premium. In theory, you can encode your MP3 files at a higher bitrate and, in the areas where there is no sound, the application will detect this and jump to the lowest possible bitrate, jumping back up to the higher bitrate when encountering sound or music. This might be good if you were listening to something along the lines of a book on tape (or CD), where there could be long silences. The best thing you can do is try it and see if it works for you.

Also, once you have set the preferences in the Record Options window, there is no need for you to go back and set them up again. Once it sounds good and you have chosen your target folder, let it be.

Encoding Multiple Tracks (Step 7)

In step 7, you encoded a single CD track to MP3. To encode an entire CD, select all the tracks on the target CD by clicking the All button next to Select Tracks to Record in the Recorder window.

The Playlist (Step 8)

The Playlist is where you assemble a number of MP3 files for playback. Tutorial 2-3 in Chapter 2 covers file management using the Music Library and Playlist in MMJB 3.0.

 Note

Blazing speed is a good thing, and with the release of MMJB 3.0, the ripping and encoding process is *much* faster than with previous versions. This is thanks to Brava Software's licensing the Xing Encoder for use with MMJB 3.0.

The Music Library

While you've got MusicMatch Jukebox 3.0 up and running, let's take a little tour of the Music Library. To make sure there is some content in your Music Library, finish ripping and encoding all the tracks from the target CD used in the previous tutorial before continuing.

Essentially, the Music Library works as your own personal MP3 database. You can add information into each or all of the MP3 or WAVE files that reside in the database. Yes, you read it right: You can put WAVE files into the Music Library as well. However, unless you have a couple of 18 GB RAID drives in your system, stick to the smaller MP3 files. To get a good look at all the features in the Music Library, you need to go up one level and expand your view (see Figure 4-28 for reference).

 Tip

On occasion, you may need to take the Music Library up or down one level in size. This is accomplished by clicking on one of the two small triangular buttons located directly to the right of Tag drop-down menu button on the Music Library.

In addition to Song Title, Album, and Artist, the Music Library enables you to enter information about each individual song (refer back to Figure 4-27). Under the headings of Genre, Tempo, Mood, Situation, and Preference, you can choose and rate each song from preset descriptions. Some of the preset descriptions are downright twisted (for example, Comatose under the category of

Mood), so check them out. Once you build up a large database of songs, these descriptions could help you (or someone else) put together a custom playlist.

Figure 4-28   The Music Library enables you to enter information about each track into the database.

Saving the Database

You may also want to create a number of custom databases. This is what the Music Library was created for. Here's all you need to do.

1. From the Options drop-down menu of the Music Library, choose Save Database As, as shown in Figure 4-29.

2. Enter the filename (**MyMusic1**, for example), and click the Save button. In the Save Database As dialog window, the extension for the MMJB Database is MMD. Your database file will be saved as "MyMusic1.MMD."

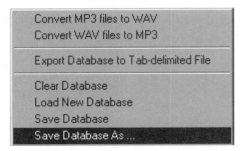

Figure 4-29   The Options menu in the Music Library gives you several options besides saving a database you've created.

Note

You can access and load existing MMJB database files by selecting Load New Database from the Options drop-down menu of the Music Library.

Tip

From the Options drop-down menu in the Music Library (Figure 4-29), you can access two separate conversion functions. These functions are (1) converting an MP3 file to a WAVE file, or (2) turning a WAVE file into an MP3. If you are into creating your own custom mixes, these conversion functions could be valuable tools.

The Bottom Line . . .

No MP3-based application fits into the all-in-one category better than MusicMatch Jukebox 3.0. It's an MP3 player, database, ripper, encoder, and tag editor all wrapped into one. If that isn't enough, you can export custom playlists and MP3 files into the Rio Player as well, although you have to take the actual memory of your Rio player into consideration with regards to the number of songs on the playlist. As far as value is concerned, MusicMatch Jukebox 3.0 is definitely worth the $29.99 retail price . . . and then some.

Note

MusicMatch Jukebox 3.0 has too many features to fit into this chapter, so refer to Chapter 1 for a tour of the Player and to Chapter 2 for the Playlist functions.

CHAPTER RETROSPECT

If you wondered which ripping and encoding application was going to be the best for you, this chapter should have helped answer all your questions. On the Windows side, we recommend both AudioCatalyst and MusicMatch Jukebox 3.0. There are more features in MusicMatch Jukebox 3.0, but that doesn't necessarily make it better, just different. Either way, you can't go wrong. On the Macintosh side, AudioCatalyst for Mac is the only commercial all-in-one application currently available.

Tip

To find out more about the latest versions AudioCatalyst for the Mac and Windows, go to `www.xingtech.com`. For more information on MusicMatch Jukebox, go to `www.musicmatch.com`.

COMING UP . . .

In Chapter 5 you'll get tutorials and a tour of the Rio Manager software, and you'll learn how to export a MusicMatch Jukebox Playlist directly into the Rio Player.

Portable MP3

5

So I will eat them in a box. And I will eat them with a fox.
And I will eat them in a house. And I will eat them with a mouse.
And I will eat them here or there. Say! I will eat them anywhere!

— *Dr. Seuss,* Green Eggs and Ham

IN THIS CHAPTER

- Rio
- VaroMan Plus
- MPMan
- MPlayer 3
- Yepp

You love MP3 and the listening choices that the related technology provides. The market potential of portable MP3 has not escaped electronics manufacturers, and they are tripping over one another to create and bring to market portable MP3 devices. Unfortunately for consumers in the United States, the RIAA (Recording Industry Association of America) has filed a number of lawsuits aimed at preventing portable MP3 devices from being sold. Nonetheless, the first-generation Rio Player from Diamond Multimedia has been on sale since November 1998, and sales are strong. In this chapter, we'll take a look at a number of products that will let you take your favorite MP3s with you wherever you go.

RIO

The Rio Player (see Figure 5-1) is lightweight, offers flawless playback, and sounds great. With Rio, you can listen to the music you choose when you're hiking, walking the dogs, at the gym, or in your car. You can hear a difference between an MP3 file and the original CD in a side-by-side comparison, but by engaging the Rio's built-in EQ and choosing the proper EQ preset (classical, jazz, or rock), the sound gets a whole lot better. When it comes right down to it, a 128 kbps (16 bit 44 kHz, stereo) MP3 file sounds better than a cassette copy of the original CD track, and it's easier to archive and transport.

Figure 5-1   The Rio PMP3000 and accessories.

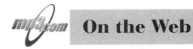 **On the Web**

You're saying to yourself, I want a Rio and I want it now. Well you're in luck. Point your browser to www.mp3.com/diamond/ and click the link to Diamond Multimedia's Rio order page.

Truth Versus Rumor

Before we get to the tutorials, it is important to let you know what the Rio does and doesn't do. There is a lot of misinformation being spread, and it is a good idea to set the record straight.

Rumor 1

First off, it has been stated that "With the Rio Player, you can download and play MP3 files from the Internet." For the record, you need a computer to act as the middleman in this transaction. At least for the time being, you cannot download MP3 files from the Internet directly to the Rio Player. In the not-too-distant future, there will be an e-commerce solution that will allow you to dock your Rio Player in a kiosk and purchase music over the Internet.

Rumor 2

The claim that one hour of CD-quality audio can be downloaded to and played back from a first-generation Rio Player is utter nonsense. The Rio PMP 3000 comes standard with 32 MB of Flash RAM, which translates into about thirty-two minutes of 128 kbps (16 bit 44 kHz, stereo) MP3 audio. An optional 15 MB Flash RAM card adds another fifteen minutes.

THE PORTABLE MP3 TAX

One of the arguments the RIAA was using in their attempt to ban the Rio Player (and portable MP3 devices in general) was that once MP3 files were loaded into a Rio Player, they could then be transferred to a completely different computer (and maybe even uploaded to a pirate Web site). Initially, this was not true, but there is now shareware and freeware that claim to make this a reality.

At some point, we consumers will be paying a tariff on the portable MP3 players that we buy, and it will go directly to the five biggest record companies. We already pay a fee of about 3 percent for each blank tape and CD we purchase for our own use.

Tutorial 5-1
NAVIGATING RIO

Before we can begin this tour and tutorial, it is important that you have your Rio hardware and software installed and in place. In this first tutorial, you will create a custom playlist in the Rio Manager and transfer it to the Rio Player.

TOOLBOX

- Windows 95/98 computer
- CD-ROM drive
- 15-pin data transfer cable

- The Rio PMP 300 Player
- Rio parallel port adapter
- Rio Manager (software)
- Rio Sampler CD or other MP3 files

 ## On the Web

The latest version of the Rio Manager software can be downloaded at the MP3.com Web site. Go to `www.mp3.com/software/windows/utilities.html`, and click on the Rio PMP 300 Software link.

GETTING CONNECTED: RIO SOFTWARE AND HARDWARE

While installation of the Rio hardware and software is beyond the scope of this tutorial, here is an overview of what each component is and how it fits into the grand scheme of things. Afterwards, if you still are confused or have questions, refer to Chapters 2 and 3 (pages 2–8) of the *Rio PMP 300 Users Guide*. There, you should find the answer to any installation question.

The purpose of the Rio parallel port adapter is to give you a place to plug in the 15-pin data transfer cable. The other end of this cable is plugged into the Rio Player, giving you a pipeline to transfer MP3 files from the host computer into the Rio Player. Once the parallel port adapter is in place on the host computer and a working Rio Player is hooked up to the computer via the data transfer cable, moving MP3 files is a software issue.

The Rio Manager software downloaded from the MP3.com Web site showed up as a self-extracting ZIP file. Clicking on the ZIP file and following the instructions and prompts makes the installation a quick and painless process. When you insert the Rio installation CD-ROM into your computer, the setup will run automatically if you are using Windows 95/98. If for some reason it doesn't, use Windows Explorer to find Setup.exe, double-click on it, and follow the installation instructions.

Note

Before you start this first tutorial, it is important to install all the proper hardware and software and to connect the data transfer cable to the Rio Player and your computer via the Rio parallel port adapter. Also, don't forget to make sure that the Rio has a fresh battery.

1. Read your manual, install all the Rio hardware and software, and insert the *Rio MP3 Music Sampler* CD-ROM into the CD-ROM drive of your computer. With all this setup accomplished, start Rio Manager.

2. Using Figure 5-2 for reference, you will note that the Rio Manager also doubles as a simple MP3 player. It is possible to open single (or multiple) MP3 files and play them back. Any file opened in the Player automatically will be transferred to the Playlist Editor. Click the Playlist Editor button to complete this tutorial step.

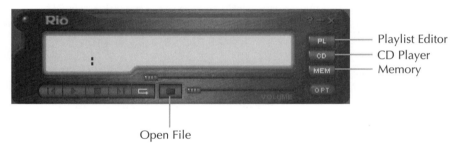

Open File

Figure 5-2   Click the Playlist Editor button in the Rio Manager Player window.

3. In this step, your objective is to add MP3 files from the *Rio MP3 Music Sampler* into the Rio Manager Playlist. In the Playlist Editor window (see Figure 5-3), click the Add button and locate the folder Tunes in the *Rio MP3 Music Sampler* CD-ROM. Then choose six MP3 files from the seventy-two or so that reside in the Tunes folder, and load them into the Rio Playlist Editor. To change the order of the MP3 files in the Playlist Editor, simply click and drag them into the desired position. When you have loaded the target MP3 files and arranged them into your preffered order, continue to step 4.

4. To save this tutorial Playlist, click the Save As button in the Playlist Editor, and select a target folder. Name the playlist **RioTest1** and click Save.

5. For this next step, you need to open the Rio Memory window by clicking the MEM button in the Playlist Editor window. This displays the current contents of the internal memory of the Rio Player. In this case, it is best to start with an empty Rio, so click the Initialize button. You will be greeted by "Initializing will delete all data. Continue?" Select Yes. This clears out the Rio's internal memory in preparation for loading the new Playlist.

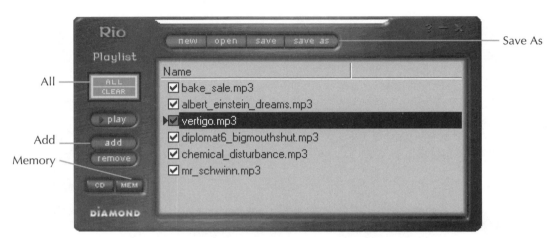

Figure 5-3   Click the Add button to load individual MP3 files into the Playlist Editor.

6. The only way to load a Playlist into the Rio's internal memory is to do the drag and drop. You need both the Playlist and Memory windows open at the same time to accomplish this task. Back in the Playlist window, click the All button (refer to Figure 5-3) to select all six of the target MP3 files. Now, click and drag all six of the files from the Playlist into the Memory window. A window pops up (see Figure 5-4) in which you can monitor the progress of the download into the Rio Player from the computer.

7. Six MP3 files now reside in the internal memory of the Rio Player. In this case, there is slightly more than 8 MB (8320 KB to be exact) of memory still remaining in the Rio Player's internal memory (see Figure 5-5 for reference). This translates to approximately eight more minutes of music that can be loaded into the Rio. To download more files to the Rio's internal memory, click the Open button and select one or more files. If the target MP3 file is too large to download, you will given the prompt "Not enough flash memory in the device." Now that there is content in your Rio, you are ready to detach the data transfer cable and go portable.

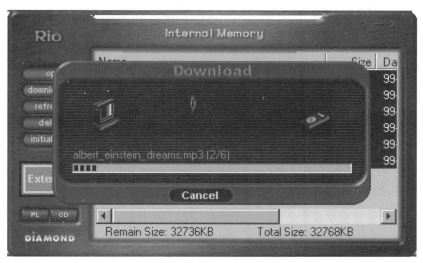

Figure 5-4   You can monitor the download progress from the host computer to the Rio Player.

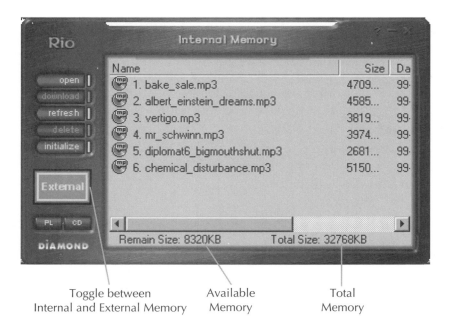

Toggle between   Available   Total
Internal and External Memory   Memory   Memory

Figure 5-5   With 8320 KB (8 MB) of memory remaining in the Rio Player, there is still room for approxamately eight more minutes of music.

Tutorial 5-1 Retrospect

Don't quit the Rio Manager just yet. First off, the Rio Manager consists of four separate components. The *Player* (refer back to Figure 5-2) allows you to preview an MP3 file and also provides the gateway to the *Playlist Editor* (PL button), *CD Player* (CD button), and *Memory* (MEM button). Although the MP3 player in the Rio Manager is pretty basic, it functions well enough and could act as the primary MP3 player on your computer.

Playlist Editor

The Playlist Editor can save and load playlists created in both the M3U and PLS file formats. In addition to using the Add button to load MP3 files to the Playlist Editor, you can drag and drop single or multiple MP3 files into the Playlist Editor as well. All of the buttons on the Rio Manager Playlist Editor are self-explanatory, and anyone with basic computer skills will have no problem understanding and accessing the functions. To rearrange the order of songs in the Playlist, simply drag them to the desired place in the desired order.

Rio Memory

The Rio Memory window is also easy to navigate and understand. While this first-generation Rio Player only has 32 MB of Flash RAM for internal memory, an optional Flash RAM card can increase the Rio's memory by as much as 32 MB. Kingston has announced the availability of 32 MB and smaller Flash RAM cards for the Rio, and other manufacturers will probably follow suit. As far as moving MP3 files into the Rio, it is much easier and quicker to create a Playlist (in the Playlist Editor) and drag all the songs over at once than to load files one at a time.

Audio CD Player

Last but not least, the Rio Manager also features an audio CD player. While there's not much to it, it works just fine. All in all, the Rio Manager software makes arranging your MP3 files and transferring them over to the Rio Player a simple process. As time goes by, there will be significant improvements in the Rio Manager software, and maybe you'll even be able to load a playlist directly into the Rio's internal memory.

Tutorial 5-2
RIO AND MUSICMATCH JUKEBOX

Brava Software, the developer of MusicMatch Jukebox (MMJB), is one of those companies that had enough vision and forethought to integrate some file-management capabilities for the Rio Player into their software. In this tutorial, we'll show you how to take a MMJB Playlist and load it directly into the Rio Player.

TOOLBOX

- Windows 95/98 computer
- CD-ROM drive
- 15-pin data transfer cable

- The Rio PMP 300 Player
- Rio parallel port adapter
- Rio Manager (software)
- *Rio MP3 Music Sampler* (CD-ROM)
- MMJB 3.0 (or higher), full version

 Note

The Rio MP3 Music Sampler CD-ROM is bundled with the Rio PMP300 package. You don't necessarily have to use this CD-ROM in Tutorial 5-2 if you already have five or six MP3 files that can be loaded into the MMJB Music Library. Please refer to "Getting Connected: Rio Software and Hardware" on page 122 before starting this tutorial. Refer to Tutorial 2-3, "Utilizing the MMJB 3.0 Music Library," if you become confused at any time during this tutorial.

1. After making sure your Rio hardware is properly connected, start MusicMatch Jukebox (MMJB) 3.0 or higher, and insert the *Rio MP3 Music Sampler* into the CD-ROM drive of your computer.

2. Click on the Clear Playlist button in the Jukebox Playlist Editor (see Figure 5-6), and then click the Music Library button on the Jukebox to open the Music Library.

Music Library   Clear Playlist

Figure 5-6   Clear the MMJB Playlist and open the Music Library to get started.

3. From the Music Library (see Figure 5-7), select Options+Clear Database. When
   prompted "Are you sure you want to clear the Database?" reply Yes and OK.

Options Menu   Add

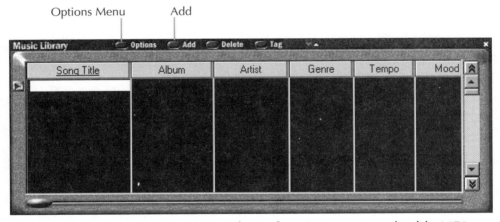

Figure 5-7   The MMJB 3.0 Music Library functions as an updatable MP3
database.

4. From the Music Library, select Add, and from the Tunes folder on the Rio MP3
   Music Sampler choose six (or more) songs to add to the Music Library database. Click OK to return to the Music Library. Note that you can add all of the
   MP3 files in the Tunes folder by clicking the Select All button. While you're in
   the Add Songs window (see Figure 5-8), you might also notice that any MP3
   files that were tagged in the Track Information window of MMJB will display all
   of the relevant information (including cover art) while in preview.

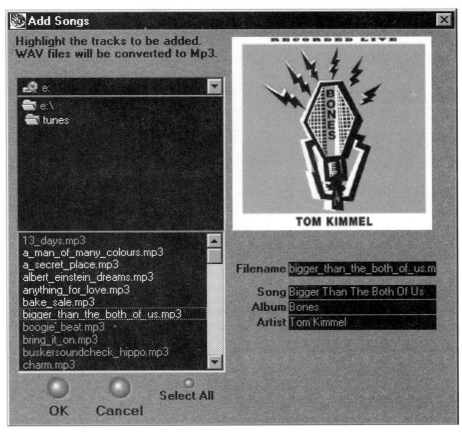

Figure 5-8   Cover art can be saved as part of an MP3 file when inserted as part of the tag in the Track Information window of MMJB.

5.   Now you should have six (or more) MP3 files in the Music Library. The task at hand is to move the six MP3 files into the Playlist. This can be accomplished by dragging and dropping the files one at a time into the Playlist. Move the target files into the Playlist (using Figure 5-9 for reference) to complete this tutorial step.

 Note

An alternate method of tranferring an MP3 file into the MMJB Playlist is to double-click on the target file while it is in the Music Library.

Playlist

Figure 5-9   Drag the target MP3 files from the Music Library, and drop them into the Playlist.

6. Now it's time to move your Playlist into the Rio Player. From the Jukebox, click the Options button, and select File+Export Playlist to Rio. During the download, you can monitor the progress as shown in Figure 5-10 and cancel all or part of the transfer. The transfer time is around thirty seconds per song. When the download cycle is complete, you will be greeted with a prompt "6 songs were downloaded into Rio." Click OK, and you're finished.

Tutorial 5-2 Retrospect

The multi-talented MusicMatch Jukebox has completely won respect by including Rio compatibility as a standard feature. For those of you not reading the book sequentially, go back and read through Tutorial 2-3 if you were confused about the Playlist and the Music Library in this last tutorial.

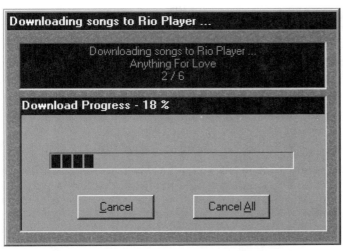

Figure 5-10   While monitoring the download progress of your MP3 files, you can cancel an individual song or cancel all of them by clicking the appropriate button.

Rio MP3 Music Sampler (Step 1)

In step 1, you were asked to insert the *Rio MP3 Music Sampler*. This CD-ROM is bundled with the Rio Player and has quite a few free promotional MP3 files. This was for those of you who didn't already have MP3 files loaded into your Music Library database. An empty Playlist and Music Library (steps 2 and 3) should have made the tutorial a lot less confusing for those of you completely unfamiliar with the Playlist and Database functions.

Music Library (Step 4)

In step 4, you were adding songs to the Music Library. When confronted with a massive number of MP3 files, load them all into the database, preview them, and delete the songs you don't like.

Loading Files into the Rio Player (Steps 5 and 6)

When moving MP3 files into the Playlist (step 5) from the Music Library, you may find it easier to just double-click the file than to use the drag-and-drop method. The choice is always yours. Also, during the actual download into the Rio Player (step 6), the Rio Manager software actually starts up and runs in the background. So you should remember that the Rio Manager software does have to be installed for the Download to Rio function to work in the MusicMatch Jukebox.

MORE PORTABLE PLAYERS

If it hasn't already started to rain portable MP3 players, it's about to. Diamond Multimedia still can't build enough Rio Players to fulfill current orders, and consumers in the United States are still hoping that one or more of the overseas electronics manufacturers will brave the threat of litigation from the RIAA and start shipping portable MP3 players. At the January 1999 Consumer Electronics Show (CES) held in Las Vegas, electronics manufacturers were showing off the future of portable MP3 devices with working prototypes as well as players that were shipping into markets other than the U.S. Following is information about a few of them.

 On the Web

To find links to the Web sites of manufacturers of portable MP3 players, go to `www.mp3.com/hardware/`.

VaroMan Plus

At the CES, Varo Vision (`www.varovision.com`) showed a working prototype of their soon-to-be-released multifunction MP3 player, VaroMan Plus (formerly known as Clicman), shown in Figure 5-11. In addition to working as an MP3

Figure 5-11
VaroMan Plus from Varo Vision integrates Iomega's Clic drive technology into a portable MP3 player and personal organizer.

player, VaroMan Plus is a digital voice recorder and electronic organizer. What really makes VaroMan Plus unique amongst the current portable MP3 devices is the integration of Iomega's new Clic drive (www.iomega.com/clik/) technology. Using 40 MB removable Clic disks as the storage medium, VaroMan Plus users can shuffle MP3 files and other data back and forth between their computers or other VaroMan Plus Players. With the estimated price of Clic disks at about $10 each, VaroMan Plus should catch on very quickly once it is released in the U.S. Data can also be transferred to and from VaroMan Plus through the parallel or USB ports of a Windows computer, and there is also a built-in speaker and numeric keypad.

 On the Web

Varo Vision has just changed the name of their Clicman player to VaroMan Plus. In addition, VaroMan, an entry-level MP3 player and digital voice recorder, was added to Varo Vision's product list. As of March 1999, Varo Vision had not made public the retail price of either VaroMan or VaroMan Plus. As more information becomes available regarding these and other portable MP3 devices, it will be posted on the update page for this book. You can get there by pointing your browser to www.mp3.com/book/ and clicking on the Chapter 5 update link.

VaroMan Plus is expected to be compatible with technology from Liquid Audio. This is a trend you will see more of in the future; it makes sense for portable music devices to be able to play music and sound from more than one format. VaroMan Plus isn't as small as the Rio Player, but it isn't any larger than an average-sized cellular phone either. While this is speculation, VaroMan Plus may be the first of many multifunctional personal electronic devices that offer music playback via MP3 technology. The integration of the Iomega Clic drive and disk combination into VaroMan Plus is sure to make this product a big seller for Varo Vision.

MPMan

Nipping at the heels of the Rio Player (at least with regards to the $199.95 price tag) is MPMan from Eiger Labs (www.eigerlabs.com/MPMan/). This first-generation MPMan (see Figure 5-12) comes standard with 32 MB of memory, but can be upgraded to a total of 64 MB, giving MPMan users as much as an hour of near-CD-quality audio playback time. The 32 MB upgrade is a factory retrofit, and your MPMan must be sent back to the factory for the installation.

Figure 5-12
The first-generation MPMan from Eiger Labs can be used as a storage device for DOC, ZIP, and EXE files as well as a playback device for MP3 files.

MPMan is powered by rechargable NiMH battery, giving the user approximately nine hours of playback per charge. Included with MPMan is a docking station that connects to the host computer through the parallel port, facilitating the transfer of MP3 files into the unit. The docking station also doubles as a battery charger.

In addition to being an MP3 player, MPMan can also be used as an external storage device for DOC, ZIP, and EXE files. This MP3 player will probably give the Rio a run for its money once it is readily available in the U.S.

MPlayer 3

Another sort of entry into the ranks of portable MP3 is the MPlayer 3 Music à la Card (www.mplayer3.com) from Pontis, shown in Figure 5-13. It appears that the MPlayer has no internal memory, meaning that music is stored on and played back from small Flash RAM cards (8 MB and larger) or ROS (Record on

Silicon) cards. According to Pontis, the ROS card is the audio storage media of the future and will soon replace the audio CD as the favored medium for delivery of music. That is hard to believe, since the point of this whole downloadable audio thing is to get away from purchasing a physical product.

Like most of the other MP3 players, MP3 files are transferred to the player through a parallel port adapter. In the case of MPlayer 3, the files are stored in the Flash RAM cards that can reside in one of two card slots. The MPlayer 3 Music à la Card looks good on paper, and when we get a chance to try one out, we'll let you know if it is worth the price of admission.

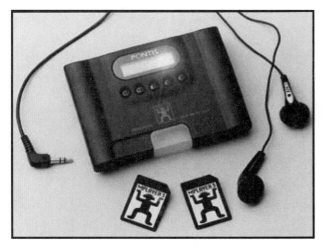

Figure 5-13   The MPlayer 3 Music à la Card uses small Flash RAM cards for storing MP3 tunes.

Yepp

Another entry into the race for your portable MP3 dollar is the Yepp (www.yepp.co.kr/) from Samsung Electronics. At this writing, there are currently three different Yepp models that will soon be offered for sale. The retail price and actual shipping dates had not been set in early 1999, but the estimated release of Yepp in the Korean market is looking like an April 1999 event.

The current top-of-the-line Yepp (the YP-D40), shown in Figure 5-14, is slated to come with 40 MB of internal Flash RAM and one slot for a YO-SM Smartmedia Flash RAM card. Appealing features are the FM stereo tuner and voice recorder integrated into the player. There is a 16-character LCD display that, among other things, may display information from the ID3 Tag of the MP3 file in play. The docking station also serves as a battery charger and parallel port interface. There is also an optional MP3 Recording Station (YO-ST) that converts and transfers CD audio into the Yepp Player. The YP-B24 model looks identical to the YP-D40 right down to the magnesium case, but lacks the FM tuner and voice-recording capabilities. The YP-B24 comes with only 24 MB of internal Flash RAM. The littlest Yepp (the YP-E16) is an entry-level MP3 Player, with no docking station. MP3 file transfers are accomplished through the parallel port of the host computer directly to the unit. Even though the YP-E16 does have a voice-recording feature, the lack of installed Flash RAM (16 MB) will probably steer most consumers to the YP-B24 and YP-D40.

Figure 5-14   The Yepp YP-D40 portable MP3 Player includes an FM tuner and a voice recorder.

At press time, there was no set retail price on any of the Yepp MP3 players. Some of the features, such as the amount of installed Flash RAM, could change as well.

 On the Web

Be sure to check the Chapter 5 update page at www.mp3.com/book/ for the latest on the Yepp and other portable MP3 players.

Auto MP3 with Empeg

There is only one automobile-based MP3 player currently in production, the Empeg Car Player (www.empeg.com). As this first-generation player is getting ready to ship, consumers can expect to pay $950 for the basic unit, without amplification or speakers. Currently, there is no photo of the production unit available, and the shipping date has been pushed back. By the time you read this, the player should be readily available — though at $950 for the basic unit, you'll *really* have to want your MP3 and have relatively deep pockets to get it.

The Empeg Car Player comes with a 2.1 GB hard drive that can be expanded to 28 GB. The heart of this computer-based MP3 player is 220 mHz Digital/Intel StrongARM processor and the Linux operating system. The player is removable, and in fact must be docked with a Windows-based PC to transfer MP3 files into its hard drive. Transfers can be made through either the parallel port or the USB port, and the base model boasts thirty-five hours of continuous CD-quality playback. Control is handled through either a credit-card sized remote control or four programmable buttons on the face of the player.

PDAs and More

It looks as if the lowly PDA (Personal Digital Assistant) is hanging out there on the fringe of MP3-land with the goal of filling the MP3 gap between the Rio-type portable and the full-blown laptop computer. With Windows CE computers and other PDAs like the Palm Pilot, we are sure to see these devices soon make inroads into the world of MP3. For the time being, the truly portable MP3 players are not going to lose any market share to PDA/Windows CE hardware. In the future, it may be a completely different story, but until the powers that be let us in on their plans with regards to MP3 and PDAs, we will just have to guess what the future has in store for us.

The MP3 Home Stereo

If you want to hook your computer up to your home stereo and don't have a clue on how it's done, there are a couple of easy ways to accomplish this task, as shown in the following sections. Your own skill level with personal electronics will dictate which method is best for you.

Radio Shack

Let's assume that you are so technically challenged that your VCR is still blinking "12:00 A.M. Sunday" and always will be. Your best bet is to call your local Radio Shack store. However, before you do this you need to estimate just how far your computer is from your stereo system. Do not do this while talking to the salesperson — do it beforehand. You should also make sure that your stereo system has an auxiliary input. You will need to ask Radio Shack to provide a cable that has a stereo RCA jack on one end (this goes into the auxiliary input) and a stereo 1/8 inch miniplug on the other end (this goes into the output jack of your computer's sound card). If your call does not go smoothly, try another Radio Shack until you get it right.

The MusicMatch Solution

The developers of the MusicMatch Jukebox sell a couple of different cables that are designed specifically for the task of channeling MP3 audio from your computer to your home stereo. Go to www.musicmatch.com and click on the 3 Connect link. From there, scroll to the bottom of the page, and you'll find the MusicMatch Cables in 100-foot and 300-foot lengths.

ONE LAST THOUGHT . . .

Portable MP3 has taken this movement beyond the computer desktop and out into the real world. Unless you're one of the five major record labels, it is only going to get better.

COMING UP . . .

If you're an unsigned musician looking to open up worldwide promotion and distribution channels for your music, Chapter 6, "MP3 for Musicians" is a must-read.

MP3 for Musicians

6

Music is the universal language of mankind.

— *Henry Wadsworth Longfellow*

IN THIS CHAPTER

- New Artist Registration
- Uploading an MP3
- We'll Do It for You
- Selling Your DAM CD
- MP3.com Artist Profiles

Almost overnight, the MP3 revolution is changing the model of the record industry, and the music industry is becoming a free-for-all. Now more than ever, the listening audience will get to decide what artists they will listen to and what they will purchase. So, for you musicians and songwriters who have a little hustle and a decent product, your chances of getting heard and selling your music are looking up. Don't quit your day gig, but the one-in-a-thousand shot you now have looks a lot better than the one-in-a-million shot it used to be. Hope is a much better motivator than desperation. Let's take a look at how MP3 is going to help you break into the music business and change the world, all at the same time. There's no better place to start than with Tutorial 6-1, "New Artist Registration."

Tutorial 6-1
NEW ARTIST REGISTRATION

The MP3.com DAM program involves filling out a few forms, uploading a few files, and you're on the air. How hard can that be? Here is a walk through the sign-up and registration process, with answers to confusing questions.

 **Note**

Getting registered as an artist in the DAM program and uploading your MP3 files and graphics are actually two separate issues. Tutorial 6-1 deals with the registration process, while Tutorial 6-2 deals with uploading the MP3 files to your artist Web site at MP3.com.

Your original music MP3 files must be encoded at a bitrate of 128 kbps (44 kHz stereo). Anything less (or more) will not be accepted by MP3.com. For more on encoding an audio or CD audio track to MP3, see Chapters 3 and 4.

TOOLBOX

• Internet-capable Windows 95/98 computer

1. Point your browser to www.mp3.com, and find Artists/Labels, as shown in Figure 6-1. Click New artist signup, and you're on your way.

2. You are now in the Artist Area – New Artist Signup (www.mp3.com/ newartist/). From here you have two options: Either click on the link go straight to Step 1, or scroll to the bottom of the page and click on the Upload the music yourself link. Because you are a "New Artist," the second option is the recommended choice. Scroll to the bottom of the page and click the Upload the music yourself link to proceed.

Artists/Labels

Artist login - Registered artists login.
New artist signup - Reach over 6 million listeners each month!
New label signup - Get more exposure for your artists at no cost!
D.A.M. signup - Create and sell CDs through MP3.com for FREE!
Artist's Messageboard - Forum for Artist's discussion and advocacy.
Band Name Generator - Need a new name for your band?

Figure 6-1   Click the New artist signup link to initiate the registration process.

 Note

MP3.com has added a new artists program called We'll Do It for You. This is for artists who do not have the means or patience necessary to encode and upload the contents of their CD to the MP3.com Web site. In the Tutorial 6-1 Retrospect, we cover the steps of the We'll Do It for You program.

3. You are now in the Artist Area – New Artist Signup – Checklist Web page (www.mp3.com/newartist/checklist.html). Initially there are two columns that require your immediate attention, Checklist for New Artists and Checklist for Individual Songs. Using Figure 6-2 as your reference, note that four items are required to complete the signup process: Band Name, E-mail Address, Genre, and an MP3 file. (Do yourself a favor and print this checklist.) As soon as you have access to these items, scroll to the bottom of the Web page and click the link Continue with Signup to proceed.

 Tip

As you saw in step 3, there are four required items you must have to successfully sign up as a new artist. There are, however, many other items you will eventually need to add to your band's MP3.com Web page. Once you have completed the basic signup process, you can go back and edit the content for your band's Web page. How to do this will be discussed in the Tutorial 6-1 Retrospect.

Q: What information do I need to have ready?
A: Here is a checklist of items you may need before you fill out the new artist form. This is a great page to print out for future reference!

Checklist for New Artists
• Band Name (REQUIRED)
• Email Address (REQUIRED)
• Genre-Rock, Techno, etc.(REQUIRED)
• Description of Music and Band, Influences
• Popular Artists You Sound Like
• History of Band, Members, Instruments
• Albums, Concert Dates, Press Releases, Extra Info
• Website, Band Logo, Picture (270 pixels width, 180 pixels height), Contact, Address

Checklist for Individual Songs:
• The MP3 file (REQUIRED)
• Song Title
• Song Description(this should be a one liner)
• CD that the song is from
• Record Label
• Song Lyrics
• Album Cover (70 pixels width x 70 pixels height)

Please note the following items:

• Duplicate band entries will be deleted.
• You MUST list an email address with your band info or your band entry will be deleted.
• Problems uploading graphics may be solved by making the graphic a few pixels larger than recommended above.
• If you intend to upload your own music, please do so immediately following artist signup.
• If you intend to participate in the We'll Do It For You program please ship your CD immediately after song signup and admin.
• Your artist information will be deleted within 60 days if you have not uploaded or sent in your music.

Figure 6-2   By reading this checklist, you can learn which items are required to complete the signup process.

4. You've now arrived at the New Band Signup – Step 1 of 5 page. You will be in for a lot of reading, but this is a very important part of the signup process. What you have before you in New Band Signup – Step 1 of 5 is a contract between yourself and MP3.com. It is important to read and understand each of the three sections of the MP3.com Music Submission Agreement. Once you have read the entire agreement and feel you understand your rights, it's time to enter the your personal information into the fields shown in Figure 6-3. By entering I Agree and clicking the button Continue to step 2, you are in fact signing the MP3.com Music Submission Agreement.

 Tip

Because you are seriously considering entering into a business agreement to promote and distribute your music over the Internet, the MP3.com Music Submission Agreement is a very important document. Print out the agreement and make sure that you have read and understand each section thoroughly before proceeding to New Band Signup – Step 2 of 5. We have recreated the entire contract for you to review offline in the Appendix.

I AM OVER 18 YEARS OF AGE: ○ No ○ Yes
I AM ACTING ON BEHALF OF THE FOLLOWING BAND (IF APPLICABLE):

MY NAME:
ADDRESS:
PHONE:
E-MAIL:

I HAVE READ AND AGREE TO BE BOUND BY THE MP3.COM MUSIC SUBMISSION
AGREEMENT:
○ I AGREE   ○ I DON'T AGREE

Continue to step 2

Figure 6-3   To proceed to New Band Signup – Step 2 of 5 you must be at least eighteen years of age and capable of entering the correct information into each field of the submission form. You must also agree to be bound by the MP3.com Music Submission Agreement.

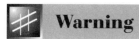 **Warning**

The information you enter at the bottom of the page in New Band Signup – Step 1 of 5 must be accurate. When you sell your music, MP3.com wants to pay you for it. If you enter bogus signup information, you won't be getting that royalty check you so much deserve. In the very near future (possibly by the time you read this), there will also be a field added for either your Social Security or Tax ID number. Entering this information will be required before you can move on to New Band Signup – Step 2 of 5.

5. Because MP3.com needs to know how and where to categorize you on the Web site, you need to fill in each and every relevant field in New Band Signup – Step 2 of 5. In this step, there are twenty-five possible fields in which to enter information. Some are optional and others, such as Band URL (shown in Figure 6-4), are mandatory. Fill in everything that relates to your band, and click the Continue to step 3 button at the bottom of the page when finished.

Band URL:

To have a custom mp3.com url of http://www.mp3.com/yourbandname, please enter a name for your band composed of only numbers and upper/lowercase letters (ie, no spaces, commas, dashes, apostrophes, etc). We recommend keeping it short (less than 20 characters).

http://www.mp3.com/ `SeizureWorld`

Figure 6-4   Create a URL for your band on the MP3.com Web site.

6. In New Artist Signup – Step 3 of 5, you review for accuracy the information you entered in New Artist Signup – Step 2 of 5. If you see a mistake that needs to be corrected, go back one step in your browser. After making the correction, click the Continue to step 3 button again. Once you are satisfied that the information in each of the twenty-five fields is correct, click the Continue to step 4 button to proceed.

7. In New Artist Signup – Step 4 of 5, you will be uploading a band photo to your MP3.com Web site. If you do not have a band photo ready to go, click the Yes, continue to step 5 button (refer to Figure 6-5). For those of you with a band photo, note that the recommended picture size is 270 by 180 pixels. In English, this means 3.75 inches by 2.5 inches. If you are going to upload your band photo now, click the Browse button to locate the file on your hard drive, and then click the Yes, continue to step 5 button to initiate the upload process. Be patient; even with a really fast connection, this could take a few minutes.

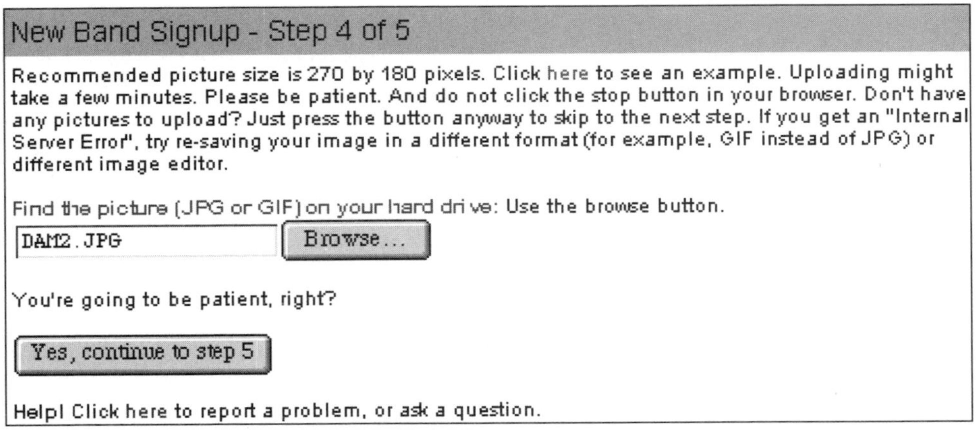

New Band Signup - Step 4 of 5

Recommended picture size is 270 by 180 pixels. Click here to see an example. Uploading might take a few minutes. Please be patient. And do not click the stop button in your browser. Don't have any pictures to upload? Just press the button anyway to skip to the next step. If you get an "Internal Server Error", try re-saving your image in a different format (for example, GIF instead of JPG) or different image editor.

Find the picture (JPG or GIF) on your hard drive: Use the browse button.

`DAM2.JPG`   Browse...

You're going to be patient, right?

Yes, continue to step 5

Help! Click here to report a problem, or ask a question.

Figure 6-5   Follow these directions to proceed to New Artist Signup – Step 5 of 5.

As you can see in Figure 6-6, by reaching New Band Signup – Step 5 of 5, you have created a Username and Password. Leave this window open, and we'll get to uploading an MP3 file to your MP3.com artist Web site (Tutorial 6-2) immediately following the Tutorial 6-1 Retrospect.

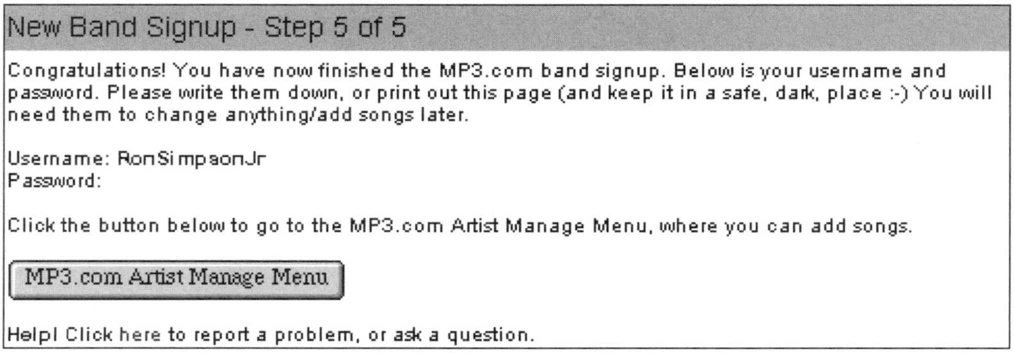

New Band Signup - Step 5 of 5

Congratulations! You have now finished the MP3.com band signup. Below is your username and password. Please write them down, or print out this page (and keep it in a safe, dark, place :-) You will need them to change anything/add songs later.

Username: RonSimpsonJr
Password:

Click the button below to go to the MP3.com Artist Manage Menu, where you can add songs.

[MP3.com Artist Manage Menu]

Help! Click here to report a problem, or ask a question.

Figure 6-6   By reaching New Band Signup – Step 5 of 5, you have a Username and Password.

Tutorial 6-1 Retrospect

There's a lot of reading and writing to go through to get signed up as a new artist. But before we upload an MP3 file, there are a few details to cover. Also, make sure not to confuse the tutorial steps with the signup steps.

Checklists (Step 3)

In Tutorial step 3 (Figure 6-2), you might find the two columns of checklist information overwhelming. In reality, you only really need the required four items (Band Name, E-mail Address, Genre, and an MP3 file) to get registered. Everything else you can enter or upload to your Web site at a later date.

Music Submission Agreement (Step 4)

Tutorial step 4 takes you to New Band Signup – Step 1 of 5. This is where you have to read, comprehend, and sign the all-important MP3.com Music Submission Agreement. This is in essence your record contract with MP3.com. It is of the utmost importance that you read and understand what you're getting into. To view the MP3.com Music Submission Agreement without going online, go to the Appendix of this book, where it appears in its entirety. Fortunately for you as an independent artist, the MP3.com Music Submission Agreement is unlike any other sales, distribution, and marketing agreement you are likely to find anywhere. It is fair; you are allowed to back out of the deal by simply giving notice; and it doesn't cost you anything to join. Still, you need to make sure that you read and understand all of the fine print of this or any document you sign. Next time around, you might not be this lucky.

Band Photo (Step 7)

Just in case there was a little confusion in Tutorial step 7 (New Band Signup – Step 4 of 5), this is where you were supposed to upload a photo of your band to your MP3.com Web site. If you currently don't have a photo that has been scanned, properly sized, and converted to either the JPEG or GIF formats, you can bypass this step for now.

 Tip

You're a musician! What do you know about scanning and converting a photo to make it Web-ready? Here's the easy solution to your problem, and all you need is a picture, a few bucks, and a Kinkos. That's right (this is not an advertisement), just about every major city has a Kinkos, and for $5 or $10, depending on your location, you can have your photo scanned, sized to 270 by 180 pixels, and converted to either a JPEG or GIF format. In short, take your picture to a professional. Alphagraphics is another easy-to-find nationwide chain that offers a similar service at a reasonable price.

 ## Tutorial 6-2
UPLOADING AN MP3

In the last tutorial, we got you registered as a new band (or artist, if you prefer), and now it is time to get one or more of your songs uploaded to your newly created MP3.com band Web page. To complete this tutorial, you must have an account with MP3.com (in other words, you must have completed Tutorial 6-1) and you must have at least one MP3 file that was encoded on a Windows computer.

Warning

There is a problem with some errant ID3 version 2 tag information that is inserted into the MP3 file when it is encoded on a Macintosh. In essence, the servers don't like content from the Mac. While there is a slight possibility this problem may be corrected by the time you read this, don't hold your breath. For the time being, MP3 files that you wish to upload to MP3.com must be encoded on a Windows computer.

TOOLBOX

- Internet-capable Windows 95/98 computer
- An MP3 file encoded on a Windows computer

1. If the New Band Signup – Step 5 of 5 window is still open (refer to Figure 6-6), click the MP3.com Artist Manage Menu button. This takes you to the heart of your own artist area in the MP3.com Web site (see Figure 6-7). From here, you can update all the information on your band's MP3.com Web site and upload or delete MP3 files from your account.

   If you are returning to the MP3.com site after having gone offline, click the Artist login link found under the Artists/Labels area (referring back to Figure 6-1) on MP3.com's main Web page (www.mp3.com). After completing the login process, you will be linked to your band's Artist Manage Menu. From there, you're ready to move on to the next step.

2. To open the Song Administration page, click the Song Admin link (refer to Figure 6-7) and then click Add New Song.

3. There are five steps to this process, the first being Add Song – Step 1 of 5, in which you will choose the proper genre for your song. Using Figure 6-8 as your reference, find the main genre that most closely reflects your song, and then click the View sub genres link. You may continue this process until you find the precise subgenre that fits your music. For example, choose Pop & Rock and click the View sub genres link. From there, choose Pop and click the link Select this genre. Once you have clicked the Select this genre link, you will automatically advance to the next step.

Welcome Seizure World!

DAM Artists please note! If we don't have a correct current address for you, we will be unable to send you a check for your DAM sales! Please use the Update Contact Info link below.

Statistics
- Artist stats Song downloads and visitors to your page.
- DAM sales Shows DAM CDs you've sold.

General
- Update artist info Change the band info on your Web page.
- Update band picture Upload a new picture of your band.
- Link admin Add/remove links to other bands on your MP3.com Web page.
- Web page preview See what your Web page will look like on MP3.com.
- Update band URL http://www.mp3.com/yourbandname.
- Update contact info Please make sure your address is correct.
- Change username and password

Song admin
Add new songs, update current ones, choose where to make them available.

DAM CD admin
Create new CDs or update current ones.

Figure 6-7   Edit the content of your band's Web site in the MP3.com Artist Manage Menu.

Add Song - Step 1 of 5

Please choose a top genre for your song:

Alternative	View sub genres
Books & Spoken	View sub genres
Children's Music	View sub genres
Classical	View sub genres
Country	View sub genres
Easy Listening	View sub genres
Electronic	View sub genres
Hip Hop/Rap	View sub genres
Jazz/Blues/R&B	View sub genres
Pop & Rock	View sub genres
World	View sub genres

Figure 6-8   Choose the genre that most closely resembles your song, and click the View sub genres link to get more specific.

Note

In March 1999, MP3.com expanded the genre categories to more thoroughly cover the diverse musical styles of the artists featured on their Web site. If your band posted material previous to this date, you may want to edit the genre category of your MP3 files to more accurately reflect the genre of your content.

4. In Add Song – Step 2 of 5, enter the name of the song and other relevant information, such as song writer and lyrics. There are nine fields of information for you to enter. Also, because of copyright law and licensing restrictions, you may not upload a cover tune to MP3.com unless you have written permission from the copyright owner to release the song over the Internet. When you have entered the relevant information, click the Continue button at the bottom of the page to move forward to the next step.

5. In Add Song – Step 3 of 5, you will select the target MP3 file you are going to upload. Using Figure 6-9 for reference, click the Browse button to select the target MP3 file, and once you locate it click the Yes, upload and continue button. At this point, you must be patient, as the upload time could be as long as an hour depending on your connect speed to the Internet.

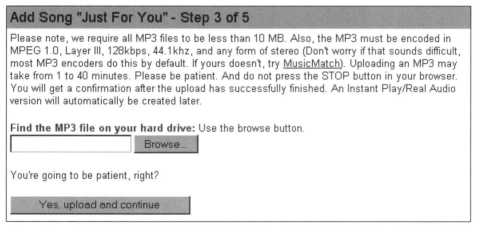

Figure 6-9   Click the Browse button to locate your target MP3 file, and once it is located, click the Yes upload and continue button to initiate the upload process.

6. Add Song – Step 4 of 5 allows you to upload a graphic of your album cover to go with the MP3 file. The graphic file must be in either the GIF or JPG format. If you don't have a graphic file ready for uploading, you can simply click the Yes, upload and continue button to move to the next step.

7. In Add Song – Step 5 of 5, you have four options. First off, if your music contains content or lyrics that would offend more conservative listeners, chances are that you should check the Parental Advisory box (refer to Figure 6-10). This will give those who might actually be concerned about what you have to say a chance to steer clear of your music altogether. In your second set of options, you get to choose who can and cannot listen to and use your song. Referring to Figure 6-10, make your choices, and click the Finish adding this song button to complete the song upload process. Remember, what you do here is not permanent. You can always go back at a later date and make an adjustment.

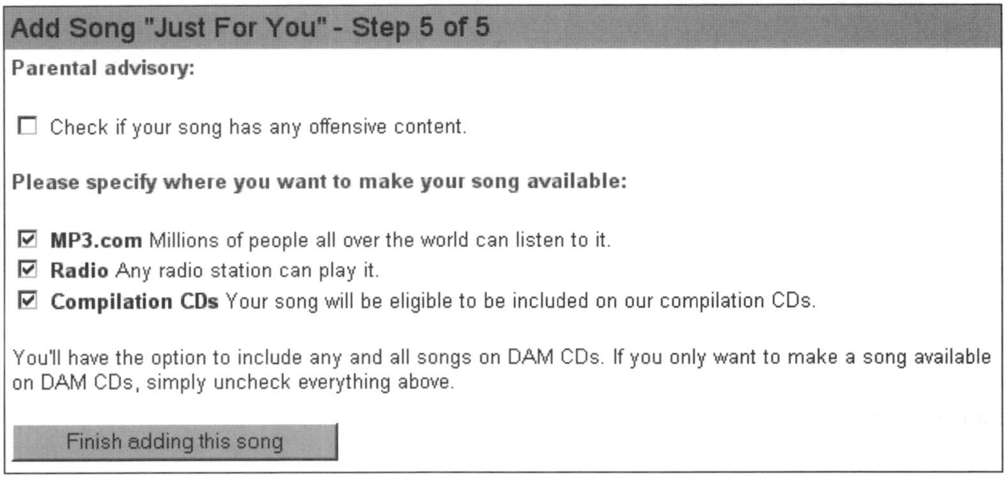

Add Song "Just For You" - Step 5 of 5

Parental advisory:

☐ Check if your song has any offensive content.

Please specify where you want to make your song available:

☑ **MP3.com** Millions of people all over the world can listen to it.
☑ **Radio** Any radio station can play it.
☑ **Compilation CDs** Your song will be eligible to be included on our compilation CDs.

You'll have the option to include any and all songs on DAM CDs. If you only want to make a song available on DAM CDs, simply uncheck everything above.

[Finish adding this song]

Figure 6-10　Your new song is now uploaded and will be ready for the entire world to hear as soon as the staff at MP3.com verifies its status.

That's it! You're uploaded, and your new song will be ready for the whole world to hear as soon as the staff at MP3.com has verified that your MP3 file was properly encoded. You can upload additional MP3 files by clicking the Add New Song link and repeating the steps of this tutorial (see Figure 6-11 on the next page).

Tutorial 6-2 Retrospect

One area that might cause some of you a little problem would be uploading or not uploading a graphic to go along with your MP3 file (Add Song – Step 4 of 5). While you might have one or more MP3 files ready to upload, it is possible that you still haven't had your album cover scanned and converted into a JPG or GIF file. This is no problem, as you can always upload the graphic at a later date. As stated in the tutorial, just click the Yes, upload and continue button and you can bypass this step altogether. Which brings me to the back to the Song Administration page. This is where you can undo any errors that you may have committed during the upload process. If you look at Figure 6-11, you will note that there are five different update links under each song (Genre, Info, MP3 file, Album Cover, and Properties). Each of these links corresponds to one of the upload steps you just completed in Tutorial 6-2. By clicking on the proper link, you can alter, adjust, and otherwise edit the content for each song you have posted on MP3.com. Be assured that any mistake you may have committed in the past can be rectified at a moment's notice.

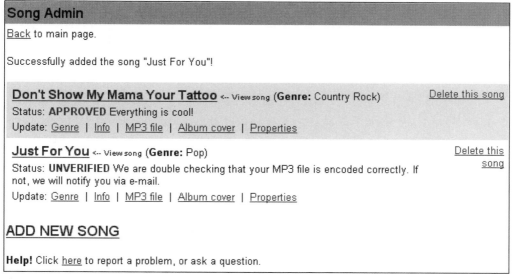

Figure 6-11   The Song Admin page displays the songs you've uploaded. You can upload additional songs by clicking Add New Song.

Quickie Tutorial: We'll Do It for You!

For those of you who feel technically challenged, don't have any ripping and encoding software, or just don't want to deal with uploading the contents of your entire CD, MP3.com has come to your rescue with the We'll Do It for You program. Following is a mini-tutorial that outlines the steps of how to take advantage of this program.

1. Your first step is to go to MP3.com's main Web page and click on the New artist signup link. From the Artist Area – New Artist Signup page, scroll down and click on the We'll Do It for You link (`www.mp3.com/cd4u.html`). Print the contents of the entire Web page for reference.

2. The next step is to go through the new artist signup process (refer back to Tutorial 6-1) to create an account with MP3.com. Once you have registered your Artist's Name and have a Password, you can log in to the registered artist's area and access your account.

3. Using Tutorial 6-2 for reference, you will need to go through the Add New Song process for each of the songs you plan to send to MP3.com for encoding. Note that you can skip steps 3 and 4 of Add New Song if you wish to add the graphics at a later date. Simply click the Yes, upload and continue button to move to the next step. Note that you must make at least one song available as a free download (this is done during Add New Song – Step 5 of 5).

4. Next, fill out the CD Mailer form (you can find it at `www.mp3.com/newartist/cd4umailer.html`). It's a good idea to print out two copies of this form and keep one in your records for reference.

5. There are three things you now need to send to MP3.com. First, your music must be sent in the form of a standard audio CD. No cassettes, no DATs, no CD-ROMs. Second, you need to send one copy of the CD Mailer form *completely* filled out. Third and final is a check for $20 in U.S. funds made out to MP3.com. These three items should be sent in a padded envelope to:

MP3.com
Attn: "We'll Do It For You"
10350 Science Center Drive
San Diego, CA 92121

Note

Once you have signed up, entered your artist info, and posted your song info, mail in your CD as soon as possible. If MP3.com has not received your CD within sixty days, your artist account with MP3.com will be deleted.

 On the Web

If you have any questions about We'll Do It for You, go to the MP3.com Support and Contact Information page at `www.mp3.com/contacting.html`. If your question can't be answered via this Web page, send an e-mail inquiry to `cd4u@mp3.com`.

MAKING SOME DAM MONEY

Sure you're artists, and you aren't really in it for the money, but it is nice get paid every once in a while all the same. The more music you sell, the greater your chances are of quitting that day gig that all musicians despise. By now, most of you have figured out that unless you're already famous, the chances of getting a record deal are probably somewhere between slim and none. Thanks to MP3.com and the DAM program (that's Digital Automatic Music), you may already be on your way to fame. If you've completed the first two tutorials in this chapter, then you're just a few minutes away from setting yourself up to make some DAM money! In Tutorial 6-3, "DAM Music for the Masses," you'll see just how quick and easy it is to create your own MP3-based CD.

 **Tutorial 6-3
DAM MUSIC FOR THE MASSES**

TOOLBOX

- Internet-capable Windows 95/98 computer
- An active artist's account with MP3.com
- Two MP3 files uploaded to your account

1. Log on to the Internet, go to `www.mp3.com/artist/login.html`, and log onto your MP3.com artist's account.

2. Click the DAM CD Admin link, and then click the Create New CD link.

3. In Create New CD – Step 1 of 2, using Figure 6-12 for reference, enter the name of your DAM CD in the first field, then choose your CD's price (between $4.99 and $9.99), pick which of your available tracks will be be on the CD, and click the Continue to step 2 button.

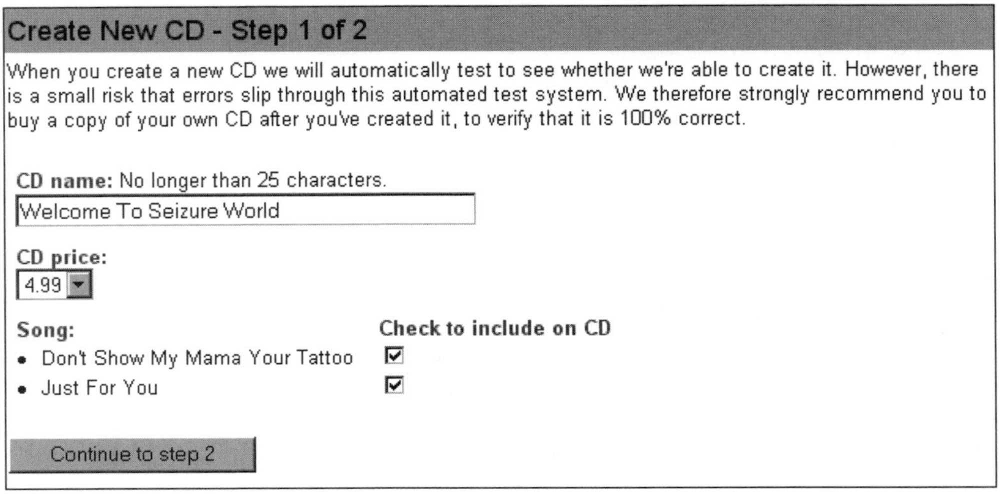

Create New CD - Step 1 of 2

When you create a new CD we will automatically test to see whether we're able to create it. However, there is a small risk that errors slip through this automated test system. We therefore strongly recommend you to buy a copy of your own CD after you've created it, to verify that it is 100% correct.

CD name: No longer than 25 characters.

Welcome To Seizure World

CD price:

4.99

Song: **Check to include on CD**
• Don't Show My Mama Your Tattoo   ☑
• Just For You   ☑

Continue to step 2

Figure 6-12   Name your DAM CD, set the retail price, and choose the songs you wish to make available for sale.

4. Create New CD – Step 2 of 2 is where you get to create the playlist for your DAM CD. Using Figure 6-13 as your reference, set the playback order of your songs, and click the Finish adding this CD button to continue.

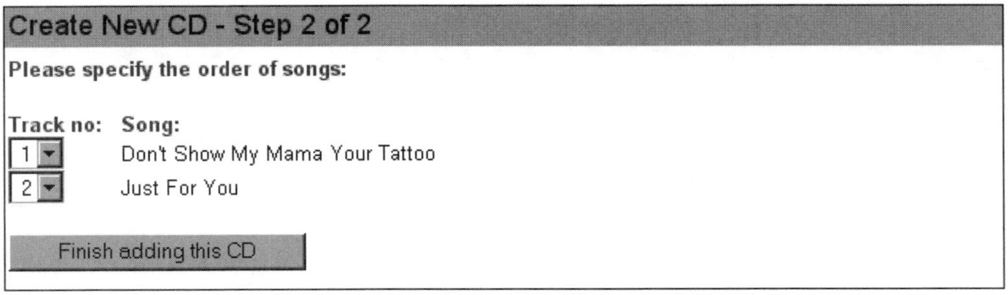

Create New CD - Step 2 of 2

Please specify the order of songs:

Track no: Song:
1   Don't Show My Mama Your Tattoo
2   Just For You

Finish adding this CD

Figure 6-13   Set the song playback order for your DAM CD.

This brings you back to your CD Admin Web page. There is one big difference, however: You now have product available for sale on MP3.com. As shown in Figure 6-14, you can update info on your DAM CD, add or delete a song, and if necessary, delete the whole CD and start all over.

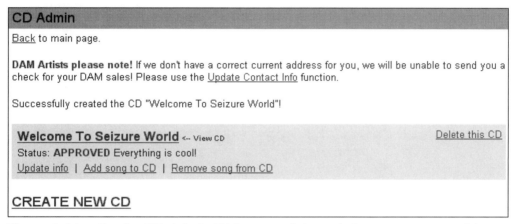

Figure 6-14   On the CD Admin Web page of the artist's area, you can add or delete content from your DAM CD.

Tutorial 6-3 Retrospect

Not only is it easy to create your own DAM CD, but updating the content on your CD and adding or deleting songs is easy as well. There is no producer or record label marketer telling you what songs are going to appear on your CD and in what order: This time it's all about you. If you've been making music for a long time, chances are you've got a lot of music already recorded and waiting for a home. Why not create two or three DAM CDs? It's up to you, and the sky is the limit.

Checking Your Stats

So exactly how popular is your music becoming on MP3.com? You can monitor the results on a daily basis. For those of you who have yet to sign up as a new artist with MP3.com and want to see how it works, here's the tour.

The first stop on this tour is the area that MP3.com has dubbed the Artist Main Menu (see Figure 6-15). From there, you can access all the information about your MP3.com artist account. In this case, we are interested in what kind of traffic your Web page has been receiving and how many times your songs have been downloaded. Under the heading called Statistics, click the link Artist Stats. From the Artist Stats page, you can view a summary of your overall traffic, downloads, and DAM CD sales on a monthly basis (see Figure 6-16). Note that there are a total of five different categories, including how many DAM CDs you have sold and your band's current overall ranking on MP3.com.

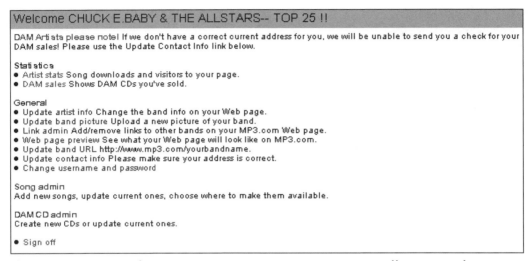

Figure 6-15 From the Artist Main Menu, you can manage all aspects of your band's account.

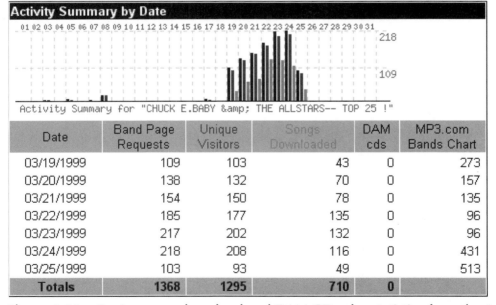

Date	Band Page Requests	Unique Visitors	Songs Downloaded	DAM cds	MP3.com Bands Chart
03/19/1999	109	103	43	0	273
03/20/1999	138	132	70	0	157
03/21/1999	154	150	78	0	135
03/22/1999	185	177	135	0	96
03/23/1999	217	202	132	0	96
03/24/1999	218	208	116	0	431
03/25/1999	103	93	49	0	513
Totals	**1368**	**1295**	**710**	**0**	

Figure 6-16 Review your download and DAM CD sales statistics from the Artist Stats page.

For those of you who wish to get a little more specific, you can also track the statistics on an individual song. Using Figure 6-17 as your reference, note that you can track the number of downloads, an individual song's chart position in its specific genre, and the song's overall position on the MP3.com singles chart. By accessing the pull-down menu shown in Figure 6-18, you can view the statistics of each individual song that is featured on your MP3.com artist Web site. If your song has shot to number one, you'll know it.

The three tutorials in this chapter show you just how simple and inexpensive it is to put your music out there in front of a worldwide audience. Now all that's left for you to do is follow through and sign up.

Song Download Summary by Date	MANANA		
Date	Downloads	Position On Latin Singles Chart	Position On MP3.com Singles Chart
03/05/1999	1	589	8109
03/07/1999	1	352	6153
03/16/1999	1	443	7897
03/17/1999	2	285	5952
03/19/1999	10	2	1130
03/20/1999	19	1	457
03/21/1999	25	1	357
03/22/1999	46	1	172
03/23/1999	44	1	182
03/24/1999	45	4	1053
03/25/1999	16	6	1452

Figure 6-17   MP3.com makes it simple to review the statistics of your individual songs.

MP3.COM ARTIST PROFILES

There's an old saying that is sort of a musician's mantra: "If I knew back then what I know now, I'd be rich and famous." Check out what these guys have to say about the music business, and see how they, along with many other musicians, are fighting to break free of a tired business model conceived by the old guard who currently run most of the big record companies. MP3.com has started a revolution that has forever changed the face of today's record industry.

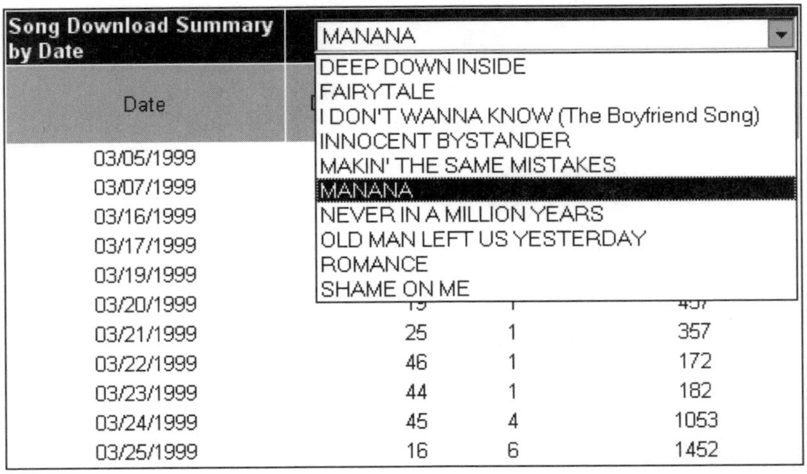

Song Download Summary by Date	MANANA ▼		
Date	DEEP DOWN INSIDE		
	FAIRYTALE		
	I DON'T WANNA KNOW (The Boyfriend Song)		
	INNOCENT BYSTANDER		
03/05/1999	MAKIN' THE SAME MISTAKES		
03/07/1999	MANANA		
03/16/1999	NEVER IN A MILLION YEARS		
03/17/1999	OLD MAN LEFT US YESTERDAY		
03/19/1999	ROMANCE		
03/20/1999	SHAME ON ME		
	19	1	457
03/21/1999	25	1	357
03/22/1999	46	1	172
03/23/1999	44	1	182
03/24/1999	45	4	1053
03/25/1999	16	6	1452

Figure 6-18   Use the pull-down menu to access the statistics of each individual song.

Michael E. Williams, "The Best Is Yet to Come"

Michael grew up in a small town in the Pacific Northwest. By the time he entered high school, Michael was doing his best to annoy most of his neighbors by loudly playing his guitar well into the night. As fate would have it, Michael moved north to Seattle and began making a name for himself as a guitarist and singer. If there was anyone who was going to make it in the music business, this was the guy. He had the drive and the talent, he just wouldn't take no for an answer, and he wouldn't compromise his music. It has been a long and interesting road that led Michael to the MP3.com artist's program. The best way to get started is to let Michael tell you in his own words.

Michael E. Williams

After years and years of singing and playing in hundreds of smoke-filled bars across the U.S., and trying to no avail to get the attention of a label, my wife Penny and I refinanced our home in Seattle and used a very large portion of its equity to finance the recording of my CD. After hundreds of hours in several of the finest recording studios the Pacific Northwest has to offer and a trip to Los Angeles for "mastering," I was confident that I had a product that the record labels would be fighting over.

　　Talk about naiveté! I spent many years of my life singing and playing on other people's projects (for the most part, on spec). And, I would always hear the words "shop it to the labels." Well, maybe in the old days, artists actually were able to get the attention of record companies by simply sending a copy of their work to the A&R department of a given label. I am here to tell you that "shopping to the labels" does not exist.

I just couldn't understand why I never received even an acknowledgment that my CD had been received. They just threw it in the trash. I met nothing but an endless series of brick walls.

Figure 6-19
Michael E. Williams.

Meanwhile, back in Seattle, I managed to get the ear of a very kind program director at a very popular radio station in Seattle. This by itself is a major feat, because big radio stations are sent literally hundreds of promotional CDs per week by distribution agents that work for the record labels. Finally, a person with the power to expose my art to the general public believed in me! Well, shortly thereafter I was on the Top 20 Best-Seller list at local record stores. Now, one would think with that kind of "sales proof," I could garner some kind of label attention.

The belief that my friend the program director had in me ran deeply. He got me into one of those posh parties that the record labels throw to schmooze program directors. (Yes, this is no bull; it really works that way.) I don't want to mention any well-known names, but I was introduced to a senior vice-president of the largest record company of the time. And, I just happened to have my promo pack in hand. Imagine that.

The very next day I got a call from Los Angeles. It was Mr. Senior VP, and he was very excited. He told me this, he promised that. I thought for sure a Grammy was right around the corner. Not! Nothing ever happened. I never heard from him again and he would never return my phone calls.

Bruised and battered, but not beaten yet, I was off to Los Angeles for a meeting with a record agent who was highly recommended. He told me this, he promised that. Sound familiar? It did to me too, and once again, I was served another large portion of BS.

I finally came to the realization that these record companies with their gofers and flack artists are simply that, BS. An artist on the outside has absolutely no control. They do only what they want to do, and much of the time it is done with lies and subterfuge. If I sound angry and bitter, it's because I am.

But lo and behold, I discovered the world of computers. Then a friend told me about an online record store called MP3.com that just might be trusted to promote and sell my CD. Wow, it was true! After auditioning my material, they immediately made my CD available for anyone who wanted to buy it. I am very flattered and happy to be there. I believe MP3.com is the answer to a prayer, spoken many times over, by thousands of artists. Now people all over the world have access to my music.

 Note

In March 1999, the title track from Michael's CD, "The Best Is Yet to Come," was featured as Song of the Day on MP3.com. The song jumped to the number-one spot in the love songs category and remained there for several days. Michael hasn't stopped smiling. Michael's artist Web page on MP3.com can be found at www.mp3.com/artists/9/michael_e_williams.html.

Chuck E. Baby and the Allstars

Chuck and the band began performing in 1986. They were a kickin' band. Chuck will tell you what has been happening.

HERE'S MY STORY AND I'M STICKIN' TO IT!

Chuck Morris — Bandleader for the Phoenix, Arizona-based band, CHUCK E. BABY AND THE ALLSTARS

Making *a living* playing music and entertaining people has been no easy task. But for the last fifteen years or so, I have been able to do just that. There is nothing more gratifying than actually getting paid for something you LOVE doing!

It took a life-changing experience (another story, another time), but when I decided to "go for it" and become a full-time performer, it took a lot of courage, and a lot of support from the people that care about me. I've been VERY lucky to have not been outta work for nearly fifteen years, thanks to the fans and clubs that believe in me.

So, by popular demand, we independently produced our first CD of original songs, entitled "Never in a Million Years," a collection of ten songs that I felt showed our versatility, and that were the most requested at live performances over the years. We made the CD for our fans, and hopefully to sell at gigs and local record stores.

Figure 6-20
Chuck E. Baby at the Rock and Roll Hall of Fame in Cleveland, Ohio.

After lining up consignment deals with the likes of Tower Records and Borders Books & Music, along with the independent record stores, locally, *we were in the record business!* The CD was well received by our fans, and we ended up with a product that we were proud of. We worked the radio stations for airplay (a nearly impossible task) and, finally, we were featured on a local rock radio show for a live unplugged performance and interview. This helped with interest in the CD locally, and we jokingly tell people that sales of our CD have climbed to "triple-plywood" in the first year!

Figure 6-21
Music from the CD "Never in a Million Years" by Chuck E. Baby and the Allstars was featured on MTV's "The Real World" and of course on MP3.com.

A Great Story . . .

About six months after the release, we were treated to a real stroke of luck. While performing at one of our most popular nightclubs, a woman came up to me and explained that she worked for a TV show that might be able to use the band's music. Now, after many years in this business, you know that I've heard it *all*. I'm thinking that the show is "Cooking with Bob" at 4 A.M. on cable. Then she tells me she's with the show "The Real World," which airs on MTV. And I'm thinking, "OK, *sure* you are." Then she gives me a cocktail napkin with a phone number, I give her a CD, stuff the napkin in my pocket — a scene replayed many times in many nightclubs *everywhere*. Well, Monday rolls around, I call the number, and lo and behold, they answer, "MTV Real World!"

It scared the heck out of me! After talking with the music department, a little negotiating, a couple of faxes, and *Shazamm!* MTV ended up licensing all of the songs. Ironic that the title is "Never in a Million Years," because never in a million years did I dream that the entire CD would be picked up by such a high-profile industry giant in such a short time! Quite a feather in the cap! This helped boost local sales, and got us great publicity, but we still couldn't garner any interest from the record industry. Because I was promoting and distributing the music on my own, I felt we needed a larger vehicle to get the music out there . . . *to be heard!*

Enter . . . the INTERNET!

The natural course of events led us to put up a page on the World Wide Web (www.chuckebaby.com). Now, I was completely intimidated by computers in general. I had little to no experience working with them. Then, my six-year-old son had computer lessons in kindergarten *and* the first grade, and I didn't want *him* to be left in the dust in this computer age. I figured that it was time to take the plunge, and break out the Visa card! A little advice from some computerized friends, a shopping spree, and I was wired!

Then gradually, I became more familiar with our home PC and discovered how *easy* it was. Pretty soon, I was pointing and clicking my way to places that I had never been before. I was certain that it would be possible to get the music to millions of people though a band Web page on the Internet. So, *with a little help from my friends*, we constructed a pretty cool Web site so that fans could get news and info on the band, listen to sound bytes, and even order our CD. When you first become computerized, you find yourself talking (a lot) about cool sites, bitchin' programs and applications, and generally becoming a nuisance in everyday conversations! But one of my fans who works in the computer industry recognized my enthusiasm and directed me to a music-based Web site that he had found by accident and thought might be of interest to me.

Discover . . . MP3.com!

I had been reading little blurbs in the media and hearing little bits and pieces from many directions about a format of digital music called MP3. I was curious, and it seemed that nobody really knew much about this new format that was getting so much attention. Then my friend directed me to MP3.com. After surfing their site, and doing a little research, I found that they were an actual digital music warehouse that allowed independent artists to place music on their site, and try to get some exposure for the music. They claimed that they were visited by music fans thousands of times a day. Well, remember, I've heard it *all*. But after reading their very simple Artist Agreement (their *deal* is that you provide a "freebie" to pique interest and, if people buy your music, they split any proceeds fifty-fifty) and figuring out that it wouldn't cost me anything, I decided to submit the music from our CD.

The process was fairly simple, even for a computer rookie like me! After downloading the "free" player/encoder, I simply ripped and encoded the music from our CD to the MusicMatch Jukebox via the CD drive on my PC. I chose the MusicMatch Jukebox, as it was recommended by the folks at MP3.com, and is easy to use. [Note: the "free" part only applied to the *player* part of the software. The upgrade for the ripper/encoder was only $29.95 and includes free upgrades as they improve.] Then, via the Internet, I uploaded the files to MP3.com for their approval. This entire process took me less than an hour! (I am lucky enough to have a cable modem through my local cable company. *If* you can get one, it's well worth it!) After approval from MP3.com, I followed the simple instructions and uploaded band photos and the CD cover artwork. A day or so later, MP3.com was hosting the band's Web site within their Web site.

Instant Success!!!

I was completely amazed by the almost *instant* response! Part of MP3.com's program allows the artist to track the action on the site. Within the first five days, we had nearly one thousand downloads from the site, and by the end of the first week, one song had shot to number 2 on the rock band chart for the entire site! By the end of the first two weeks, we had over 2,100 downloads of our music, and the band had moved to number 25 for the genre! And that was by doing *absolutely nothing*! If a working band could promote the fact that their music is available at MP3.com, the possibilities are mind boggling!

Where to NOW?

The newness of our music on the MP3.com site has worn off a bit, but we are still getting a lot of hits on the site (hundreds, instead of thousands). My feeling is that it is a viable and wonderful place for independent music to be heard. The music/record industry is in flux and disarray, and MP3.com is in the right place at the right time. I am anxious to attend the MP3.com summit this summer to stay abreast of all the new developments in this exciting time for digital music.

In the meantime, it's business as usual! I'll continue to work in this crazy music business, doing my eight gigs a week, selling my CD off the stage, and loving every minute of it!

Note

Chuck E. Baby and the Allstars can be found on the Web at www.chuckebaby.com or on MP3.com at www.mp3.com/music/Rock/5892.html. In March 1999, Chuck E. Baby and the Allstars opened up for Cheap Trick and will soon be playing at Alice Cooper's new bar, Cooperstown. One of the songs from their DAM CD, "Mañana," reached number one four days in a row in the Latin category on MP3.com. Chuck is still out there playing music, eight days a week.

BEFORE WE GO

There are probably a thousand different ways to market your music over the Internet, and the options grow on a daily basis. For the entry-level recording artist, there is no better place to make your music available to millions of people worldwide then MP3.com. If you have a little marketing savvy and don't mind sending out e-mail to everyone you know (don't be calling it "spam"), you can help generate even more traffic at your band's MP3.com Web site. The more people who hear about you or your band and show up at your Web site, the more DAM CDs you are going to sell.

For all you musicians, songwriters, and producers who have had little or no success in breaking into the exclusive club that is currently being run by the five major record labels, you could not have chosen a better time or place than MP3.com to let the world hear what you have to say. By opening an artist's account and uploading your music to the MP3.com Web site, your music can be for sale to an ever-expanding global audience in just a day or two. If you have new music to add to your DAM CD, all you need to do is upload it, and your latest release will be available worldwide in less time then it takes to send a letter through the U.S. mail. Whether you are just starting out in the music business or are a seasoned veteran with a long list of recording credits under your belt, MP3.com truly offers your best chance to be heard by millions of people.

In the Chapter 7 you'll be getting a look at the so-called competition to MP3 as well as a preview of a new coalition that is sure to legitimize the sale of downloadable MP3 files.

Competition and Coalitions

7

If it looks like fud, and it smells like fud, it's probably fud.

. . . This term is common computer industry lingo for a special set of tactics [fear, uncertainty, doubt] used by monopolies to stifle and subvert competitors.

— Michael Robertson

IN THIS CHAPTER

- AAC
- a2b music
- Madison
- Liquid Audio
- MP4
- MS Audio 4.0

- RealAudio
- Sony
- Sound VQ
- SDMI
- Genuine Music Coalition

Not too long ago, the record industry was up in arms against any individual or company involved with the MP3 movement, and lawsuits were being filed at the drop of a hat. It is a little quieter now, and everyone in the online music community is hard at work trying to create a successful business model using MP3 and several other similar formats. As to what will happen in the long run, it is anybody's guess, but when the dust settles, the consumer will more than likely have a lot more options when it comes to buying and listening to music. In this chapter, we're going to give you an overview of a few of the major players in this online free-for-all. Companies that were once touting what could be called a competing technology are fast incorporating MP3 (or MP3-like features) into their business models.

THE COMPETITION

It's a war, and there will be no prisoners. The question is: Who will win? Hopefully, the answer will be, Music fans and recording artists. There are a number of so-called competitors to MP3, but the fact is that this is more than a format war, it's a popularity contest as well. In addition, there are security issues involved. Music delivery over the Internet changes weekly. The following sections overview what is currently being offered by the music-technology community in hopes of winning your download dollars. It would be out of place to say that one technology is better than another. For all we know, some of these companies may have a change of heart and integrate MP3 into their existing lineup. As always, it's up to you, the consumer, to make the call about what's best for you.

AAC

AAC (Advanced Audio Coding) is the latest MPEG standard on perceptual coding and is being touted as the next generation of MP3. The developers of AAC include the Fraunhofer Institute (the developers of the original MP3 spec), AT&T, Dolby Labs, and Sony. Currently, a2b music and Liquid Audio have integrated the AAC codec (encode and decode technology) into their proprietary audio formats, and it is a sure bet that others will follow. AAC is based on MP3 and is actually the next step in the development cycle, offering a higher compression ratio and improved sound quality over MP3. Because of the buzz being created in the press about MP3, companies using AAC are now calling it MPEG AAC.

So, if MPEG AAC is the next generation of technology and it sounds better than MP3, does this mean MP3 is now obsolete? Not at all. MP3 still sounds good, and, since it is an open standard without the restrictions imposed on emerging technologies such as MPEG AAC, chances are that people will continue to use MP3. We are already beginning to see AAC being used by companies like a2b music and Liquid Audio, and it's only a matter of time before portable MP3 players become compatible with this newer format as well as MP3. When it comes down to it, because of the availability of ripping and encoding software in the MP3 format, no matter how great any of the new compressed audio formats may sound, MP3 will probably remain the people's choice.

a2b music

So who are these guys, and what exactly is it that they're selling? a2b music (`www.a2bmusic.com`) is an offshoot of AT&T and, in theory, is a competitor for Liquid Audio. Can you buy any music downloads from a2b music? Yes, as of early 1999, several record labels are offering downloadable tracks for sale using the a2b music version of MPEG AAC.

a2b Playback

Currently, the only option for playback of a2b music files is the a2b music player (see Figure 7-1). This player is a free download and can be found at `www.a2bmusic.com`. Like Liquid Audio, the a2b music player is compatible with both Windows (95/98 and NT 4.0) and Power Mac computers. Unlike Liquid Audio, a streaming preview is not possible with version 1.0. However, with the release of the a2b music player 2.0 in Spring 1999, streaming previews will be an added function. At this time, none of the popular software-based MP3 players (Sonique, Winamp, and so forth) are able to play an a2b music file.

Encoding

There are essentially two options for those wishing to encode their audio content into a2b music's MPEG AAC. First off, Encoding.com (`www.encoding.com`) has signed an agreement with a2b music to exclusively handle all their encoding chores. Because the a2b music encoding software is not commercially available, the second option would be to license the software from a2b music. There is currently no set fee for this license, and by all rights, it could be very expensive.

The sound quality is very good. The a2b music player works well on both Power Mac and Windows 98 computers, and without a hiccup or a glitch in playback. Currently, there isn't a whole lot of content available for sale in the a2b format, and there are very few preview tracks available. While the downloadable tracks from a2b music sound really good, it is questionable whether consumers are going to be willing to download yet another player and adopt another format with so little content available. Nevertheless, MPEG AAC does sound good.

Figure 7-1   In addition to playing music, the a2b music player is a repository for a song's credits, lyrics, and cover art.

Madison

It's top secret, it uses an unidentified encryption scheme, and it isn't clear exactly what Madison is or does. Sure there have been rumors, but the facts about Madison have yet to trickle down to the mainstream press.

The Madison Project has been under development by IBM and the big five record companies and is currently being beta tested in the San Diego area. Lots of hardware and a high-speed Internet connection seem to be required. It also would seem that getting the music the way you want it is not part of the plan. As it now stands, around two thousand commercially available CDs will be available for download over a high-speed cable modem and, with a CD burner, Madison users can create their own CDs. The cover art for these CDs is also available for download and can be printed out as well. Sounds pretty good so far, right? Well . . . the user cannot alter the playlist in any way, shape, or form. This essentially means that you are purchasing or leasing a bunch of hardware so that you can make your own custom audio CDs that are the exact duplicate of what you can already buy in the store or online. Unless you have a color laser printer, the cover art will probably end up looking like a cheap knockoff of the original. And even if the sound quality is as good as what you will find on the commercially released CD, you have no choice about the order of playback of the tracks. From a commonsense standpoint, you would be better off buying a CD from a retailer. Maybe this is the point the record labels are trying to get across with the Madison Project. Singles will be available for download, but the consumer will only be able to choose from a list that is made available by the record companies. Again, if you want to have it your way, you are out of luck.

One of the claims of the Madison Project is that consumers will be able to download sixty-minutes worth of music in ten minutes using high-speed cable modems. In theory this is true, but in reality very few cable modem systems perform close to their advertised speed, especially when the network is clogged with a lot of people downloading large files.

There were rumors that the formation of SDMI (the Secure Digital Music Initiative) was essentially the death of the Madison Project, so it was quite a surprise to hear that the preliminary six-month evaluation (beta test) in San Diego was going to proceed. Whether Madison will ever make it to market (so to speak) is another question altogether.

 On the Web

If you're looking for any online information about the Madison Project, for the time being, you are out of luck. However, as soon as something breaks, we'll post it at www.mp3.com/book/.

Liquid Audio

With regards to delivering near-CD-quality music over the Internet, Liquid Audio (www.liquidaudio.com) is the undisputed pioneer. Formed in 1996, Liquid Audio was the first company to actually develop and implement a working model for secure delivery of downloadable digital music over the Internet. The record industry was no more happy about Liquid Audio back in 1997 than they are about the proliferation of MP3 today.

The Liquid Music System

The Liquid Music System (currently in version 4.0) consists of three main components: the Liquid Music Player, the Liquifier Pro, and the Liquid Music Server. The Liquid Music Player (see Figure 7-2) is available as a free download from the Liquid Audio Web site and offers many features that were designed with e-commerce in mind. Information such as cover art, liner notes, and lyrics are available by clicking the corresponding buttons on the Liquid Music Player. Another feature of the Liquid Music Player is the ability to burn a custom CD from the playlist (click the Tracks button) with no additional software (although a compatible CD-ROM burner is required). The Liquid Music Player offers streaming audio previews of content over the Web. Because of scalable technology, the Liquid Music Player adjusts the sound quality to match the speed of each individual user's Internet connection. The majority of the streaming previews are about thirty seconds in length, although many artists are opting for full-length previews that are also available as free downloads. In comparing the sound quality of a streaming Liquid Track to that of a RealAudio file, the Liquid Track will win every time.

The Liquifier Pro is the second component of the Liquid Music System. While the primary purpose of the Liquifier Pro is to convert standard AIFF or WAVE files into a Liquid Track, security and digital watermarking features are also included. In addition to using a licensed version of the MPEG AAC and Dolby Digital audio formats, the Liquifier Pro is expected to add MP3-compatibility within the system soon. Another Liquifier Pro feature is the ability to insert an expiration date into a Liquid Track during the encoding process. This makes it possible for the artist and label to give away a free Liquid Track and set an expiration date to coincide with a CD release.

The Liquid Music Server is the third component of the Liquid Music System. The server handles all of the e-commerce functions, as well as the rights reporting. When a Liquid Track is sold online, the Liquid Music Server records the sales information for the songwriter, music publisher, recording artist, and record label. Each party entitled to a piece of the pie gets paid accordingly. Currently, the only way to stream a Liquid Track preview over the Web is with the Liquid Music Server.

The Liquid Future

Initially, Liquid Audio was perceived by many in the MP3 community as competition or even as the enemy. This is no longer the case. With the formation of the Genuine Music Coalition (covered later in this chapter) and the integration of the MP3 format into a future version of the Liquid Music System, it's clear that Liquid Audio has chosen to move forward with the times and let the consumer make the decision about which format to listen to.

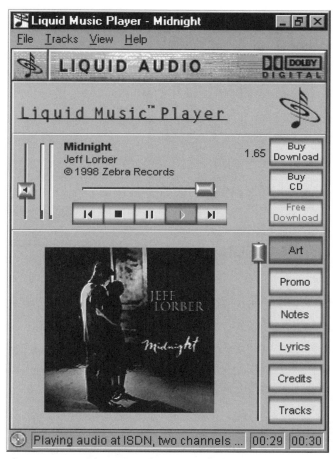

Figure 7-2 The Liquid Music Player 4.0.

MP4

Just when we were getting comfortable with MP3, along comes MP4. So if MP3 sounds good, does that mean MP4 sounds really good? The answer would have to be that it does, but a complete answer ends up being a little more complicated than just audio quality. Note that we are not talking about MPEG-4 here, but MP4.

What Is MP4?

Touted as the next generation in digital audio technology, MP4 was launched by GMO (Global Music Outlet) in early January 1999. For many, this was confusing, and for good reason. This MP4 is not MPEG-4 but a derivative of MPEG AAC. Also, unlike MP3 (MPEG-1 Level 3), this particular flavor of MP4 needs no separate player. When the user downloads the MP4 file, it shows up as a self-executable EXE file. By clicking on the EXE file, the self-contained player launches and the music begins. MP4 has a compression ratio of 16:1 (versus MP3's 12:1) and claims better sound quality than an MP3 file as well.

 Note

For MP4 to work, you must be using a Pentium 133 mHz (or faster) Windows 95/98 computer. So far, there is no MP4 for the Mac.

If you're curious as to how MP4 sounds, fire up your computer, and point your browser to mp4.globalmusic.com. From the main Web page on Global Music Outlet's site, just follow the link to the MP4 download page, choose a song, and download it to your hard drive. Using Figure 7-3 as your reference, notice that there are three file options. The first, GET MP4, allows you to download the entire file to your computer. The second, GET MP4/20, lets you download a twenty-second preview. And the third, SEND MP4/20, allows you to e-mail an

Figure 7-3   Download a full-length MP4 file, an MP4/20 (twenty-second) preview, or e-mail an MP4/20 to a friend.

MP4 preview to an interested friend. The MP4 file is about 30 percent smaller than an MP3 file of similar duration. Note that you must save the file to your hard drive rather than trying to open it from its location on the Web. It will show up on your hard drive as an EXE file. By clicking on the EXE file, you will launch a self-executing MP4 player (see Figure 7-4) and playback of your MP4 file will automatically begin. Within this self-contained MP4 file and player, the user can adjust the volume (in stereo, no less), play, pause, or stop the music, and link to the artist's home page by clicking on the album cover art.

Global Music Outlet's version of MP4 is a handy promotional tool for the independent recording artist. The downside is that whenever you want to hear an MP4 song, you have to launch an individual file. For those used to loading a bunch of songs into a playlist and listening, Global Music Outlet's MP4 format ends up being more trouble than it's worth. It does sound good, though. Will it replace MP3? Not in its present form.

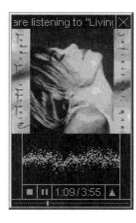

Figure 7-4
Global Music Outlet's self-executing MP4 player.

 Note

Again, for those of you who missed it the first time around, Global Music Outlet's MP4 is *not* MPEG-4, it is a derivative of MPEG AAC. Now for a really weird twist, according to the recently released specs on MPEG-4 version 1, MPEG AAC will be a part of MPEG-4. This means that MPEG-4 players should be able to decode and play AAC files. Only time will tell.

Microsoft

Microsoft has announced the release of MS Audio 4.0. This is a new file format that claims to compress an audio file to about half of the size of an MP3 file while providing superior sound quality. Microsoft has not yet indicated what features we can expect to see and hear. Microsoft's audio entry will make the game a little more interesting.

 On the Web

Point your browser to `www.mp3.com/book/` to find the latest information on Microsoft Audio 4.0.

RealAudio

RealNetworks (`www.real.com`) has without a doubt cornered the market on delivering streaming content to the masses over the Internet. Instead of positioning themselves as competition to MP3, they've come out looking more like a strategic partner instead. There's no place where that is more evident than the MP3.com Web site. Before downloading a free MP3 file from the artist's area of MP3.com, visitors are given the option of first listening to an instant-play streaming RealAudio version (see Figure 7-5) of the target track. If what you hear isn't exactly what you were looking for, then you have saved the time of a download thanks to this preview.

Recently, a streaming MP3 option has been added to the RealPlayer G2 in the form of a plug-in from Digital Bitcasting Corporation (`www.bitcasting.com`). This plug-in is a free download and works with both streaming MPEG video and MP3 audio over the Internet. While most of you probably wouldn't consider using the RealPlayer G2 as an MP3 player, the playback is smooth and the sound quality is quite good when using Digital Bitcasting's MPEG plug-in in conjunction with the RealPlayer G2.

For content providers wanting to deliver high-quality streaming MP3 to their customers, the combination of the RealServer G2 software with the MPEG G2 software from Digital Bitstream is going to be your ticket to success. Download the free RealPlayer G2 and the MPEG plug-in from Digital Bitstream, and you will hear some of the highest quality streaming audio found on the Internet. The RealPlayer G2 is definitely becoming a part of the MP3 revolution. As this multiformat player continues to mature, you can count on seeing more features that will be attractive to the MP3 community as a whole.

The Best Is Yet To Come
Get MP3 (4.4 MB) Instant
Play Song lyrics
Description: R&B Love Ballad
CD: Michael E. Williams, The Best
Is Yet To Come Label: Silver Star
Productions Inc. Seattle Wa.
Credits: Written by: Tim Scott.
Produced and performed by: Michael
E. Williams

Available on DAM CD (DAM CDs include audio tracks +
MP3 files)
The Best Is Yet To Come for only $8.99

Figure 7-5 At MP3.com, you can hear a RealAudio streaming preview of the target MP3 file by clicking the Instant Play link in the artist's area of the site.

Note

Providing streaming MP3 content via the RealPlayer G2 is not free. To broadcast streaming MP3, you will need to purchase server software from RealNetworks and Digital Bitcasting Corporation. Hanging out on the cutting edge has its price.

Sony

What Sony seems to have up their sleeves looks to be a little less format-specific and a little more up the alley of copy protection and encryption. While it is still early to know whether Sony is going to be using MP3, AAC, VQF, or some yet-to-be-invented codec for the delivery of music files, Sony seems poised to enter into direct competition with a2b music and Liquid Audio with a complete solution that includes the hardware and software.

The first level of Sony's encryption technology has been dubbed "MagicGate" and "OpenMG." While little hard data were actually available at press time, it seems that this technology supports moving encrypted data between a personal computer and compliant audio players and recorders. The trick here is that the files are moved, not copied. Even if it is intercepted in transit (over the Internet, for instance), an unauthorized user is out of luck because the data is encrypted. You can count on Sony to implement these technologies into their line of PCs and the soon-to-be-released Memory Stick.

Moving one step up with Super MagicGate, Sony is developing a secure media distribution system that will no doubt rival a2b music and Liquid Audio. In fact, Super MagicGate looks conceptually a lot like the business model that Liquid Audio has had up and running for the last two years. The big difference here is that Sony owns a lot of music content (Sony Records), manufactures music playback devices in about every format known on the planet, and manufactures computer hardware and related peripherals. Sony plans to present their complete technology package to SDMI (Secure Digital Music Initiative) for approval and then license the technology to all takers. While there are many partial solutions to delivering digital music in a secure fashion, regardless of which format (or formats) that Sony ends up presenting to consumers, it looks as though they have everything needed to bring their business plan to market. In the long run, how will this effect MP3 users? It will depend on the cost to the consumer of implementing all the related technologies, and of course whether we end up getting the music we want, the way we want it.

Twin VQ/VQF

Twin VQ technology from Nippon Telegraph and Telephone (NTT) has been nipping at the heels of MP3 as of late with a very strong following in Japan and Europe. Twin VQ (transform-domain weighted interleave vector quantization) audio compression technology was developed by NTT Human Interface Laboratories and is said to have better sound quality than MP3 with its compression ratio of 18:1 (in comparison to MP3's 12:1). In theory, a comparable VQF file is 50 percent smaller than its MP3 counterpart, with similar or even better sound quality, if you believe the claims made by NTT.

Twin VQ is available from Yamaha (www.yamaha-xg.com), using what Yamaha calls Sound VQ. Sound VQ files (VQF) can be downloaded and played back locally from a hard drive, or streamed over the Internet and played back with either the Sound VQ Player (see Figure 7-6) or via Sound VQ plug-in. Currently, the Yamaha Twin VQ technology is still in beta testing. It will work with either Power Macintosh or Windows 1995 or later computers. Windows NT 4.0 compatibility is being implemented. The exception is the Sound VQ plug-in, which is now Windows-only.

Yamaha also offers a free beta version of the Sound VQ encoding software (for Mac and Windows). It appears that the only reason it is still being called beta software is because they are not sure whether they should sell it or give it away. The beta software expires every few months, and you have to download a more current version. When used for Web-based streaming audio projects, Sound VQ seems to sound better and play with fewer problems than RealAudio. The overall popularity of MP3 dwarfs that of Sound VQ, but you never know what the future will bring. Beauty is in the eyes (or in this case, the ears) of the beholder, and right now the majority of the world is listening to MP3.

Figure 7-6
The Sound VQ Player from Yamaha is compatible with Windows and Power Macintosh computers.

COALITIONS

A couple of different coalitions have been formed as the result of MP3's popularity. In essence, SDMI (the Secure Digital Music Initiative) was formed with the express purpose of coming up with a record industry solution to the lack of copy protection on MP3, while GMC (Genuine Music Coalition) was formed to help legitimize MP3 sales as a viable and legal form of e-commerce. What follows is a brief overview of each of these coalitions.

SDMI

Once upon a time, there was a monopoly. After a few corporate mergers and buyouts, the majority of all recorded music was under the control of five multinational companies. Profits were up, and life was good. The industry was looking toward implementing DVD as the new high-quality standard, and even higher profits. The official organization that represents the interests of the record industry in such matters as lobbying Congress for changes in the laws is the Recording Industry Association of America (RIAA). The initial reaction to MP3 by the RIAA was strict condemnation in the mainstream press. As time passed and more and more people started using MP3 to listen to music on their computers, the record industry started getting nervous. Enter SDMI.

The formation of SDMI was announced at a press conference in New York City on December 15, 1998. Heading up SDMI was the RIAA, but many other technology-based music and computer companies jumped on board as well. With a basic membership fee of $10,000 for the first year, it wasn't going to be cheap to join. If you wanted to have any real input, it cost $50,000 to get a seat on the steering committee.

While the proliferation of illegal MP3 files on the Internet is probably why SDMI exists, SDMI isn't there to stamp out the use of MP3. Many members would like nothing more than to see the MP3 format disappear into obscurity, but this isn't going to happen. The issue here is security and control of content. What SDMI is hoping to accomplish is to create a set of industry standards for the sale and distribution of downloadable digital music. This does not necessarily mean a music-industry-approved replacement for MP3, but something more along the lines of a series of guidelines that the record industry will then adopt.

Since many of the major players in SDMI have invested a considerable amount of time and money into developing hardware and software that will meet their needs, it is highly unlikely that any one format or technology will emerge as the standard that all members will use. Instead, a set of standards will probably be implemented that will work equally well with a variety of technologies. Because the power players involved in SDMI are concerned about portable playback devices such as Diamond Multimedia's Rio Player, there will probably be some sort of broad-based encryption standards that will eventually be adopted by hardware manufacturers to please the record labels.

A number of companies are lobbying to get SDMI to adopt their encryption and digital watermarking technologies as the standard used by all SDMI members. Sony, IBM, AT&T, and some smaller companies all have software and hardware solutions ready to go. No one in this business is naive enough to believe, for example, that Sony would roll over and agree to accept IBM's Madison as the de facto standard. The politics and battle for future market share of hardware and software (not to mention the music) amongst the major players in SDMI will, more than likely, prevent the implementation of an effective set of standards any time soon. In the meantime, consumers will just keep using MP3.

Genuine Music Coalition

Soon after the formation of SDMI, Liquid Audio (a member in good standing of the SDMI steering committee) took it upon themselves to form the Genuine Music Coalition (GMC). Along with forty-eight other companies, Liquid Audio formed GMC for the specific purpose of making technology available to coalition members to identify and authenticate the origin of online music.

Figure 7-7
The Genuine Music mark will be displayed on
the Web sites of all GMC members selling MP3
files over the Internet.

GMC has no intention of trying to create or introduce a standard for encryption of MP3 files. They just want consumers and recording artists to be assured that MP3 files purchased from an e-commerce Web site displaying the Genuine Music mark are authentic and authorized (see Figure 7-7). To make sure that legitimate MP3 sales thrive over the Internet, Liquid Audio is working to develop technology components that will permit coalition members to easily integrate the Genuine Music mark into their MP3 content. Liquid Audio's proprietary digital watermarking technology is expected to be available to coalition members soon.

For the record, MP3.com is a member of GMC.

LOOKING FORWARD

If we were in school, you'd be getting a pop quiz on Chapter 7 right about now. Instead, we're going to move forward to Chapter 8.

8

The World According to MP3

MP3 is following a similar development path [to DOS]. It clearly has its faults, but the technology seems to suffice for most. It fills a great need at a time when there are few choices. Much like DOS, it provides a foundation which others can build upon.

— *Michael Robertson*

IN THIS CHAPTER

- The Origins of MP3

- How Does MP3 Work?

- MPEG-7

For those who make a living working with music and sound, the debate over whether analog sounds better than digital audio or vice versa will continue to be a topic of discussion for many years to come. Beauty, they say, is in the ear of the beholder. In this chapter, we're going to explore MP3 in a layman's sort of way, debunk a few myths about this popular file format, and give you some useful information at the same time.

CATCH A WAVE!

At some point in the 1980s, it appeared that computers and music were on a collision course and there was nothing anyone was going to be able to do to stop this from happening. In the world of audio, the Macintosh ruled, while the Atari,

Amiga, and DOS computers battled it out for a distant second place. Hard drives were small and very expensive, and a computer with 4 MB of RAM was considered a heavyweight machine. Then along came the Windows OS, which ran on top of DOS, and which looked much like Mac OS. As Windows matured beyond 3.1.1, WAVE files (.WAV) became the audio standard for the Windows platform, and many audio files were in fact WAVE files before they were converted into the audio CDs that many people listen to today. To be considered of CD-quality, a WAVE file would have to be 16-bit, 44 kHz stereo. This size WAVE file would take up slightly more than 10 MB of space for every minute of duration. With a five-minute song taking up 50 MB of disk space, it wasn't practical to post music on a Web page and share it with your friends. However, this would change.

WHAT DOES MP3 DO?

MP3 allows us to shrink the size of a standard WAVE file (or AIFF on the Mac) by a factor of 10, while still maintaining much of the overall sound quality. In the last section, we referred to a five-minute CD-quality stereo song in the WAVE format taking up approximately 50 MB of disk space. When that same WAVE file is encoded as a 128 kbps stereo MP3 file, it takes up only 5 MB of disk space. In short, you can store ten five-minute MP3 files in the same disk space that can hold only one five-minute CD-quality WAVE file. As this became obvious, the underground popularity of MP3 took off like a rocket.

THE DEVELOPERS OF MP3

In 1987, the Fraunhofer Institute in Germany went to work on perceptual audio coding and eventually devised the very powerful compression algorithm that we now know as MP3. *MP3* is an acronym for MPEG-1 Layer 3, and the term *MPEG* itself is an acronym for Moving Picture Experts Group, which is the name of a group of standards used for coding audiovisual information into a compressed digital format. Of the three layers of MPEG-1, layer 3 is the standard for coding audio. The final set of standards for MPEG 1 (layers 1, 2, and 3) were approved in November 1992.

Two companies hold the majority of the patents for the MP3 technology, The Fraunhofer Institute and Thomson Multimedia. The Fraunhofer Gesellschaft, based in Munich, Germany, is the leading research organization in Germany, with forty-seven research facilities throughout that country. Specifically, the Fraunhofer Institut Integrierte Schaultungen (Fraunhofer IIS), based in Erlangen, Germany, has been where much of the development work for the audio coding schemes in MP3, MPEG-2 AAC, and MPEG-4 took place. On the other hand, Thomson Multimedia (we know them as RCA) is the fourth largest consumer electronics company in the world. These two companies have split the licensing of their patents into two areas, with Thomson Multimedia handling the consumer end of MP3 licensing and Fraunhofer handling professional applications.

In theory, anyone who develops and sells (or gives away) an MP3-based product that uses any of the proprietary code on which the Fraunhofer Institute and Thomson Multimedia own the patents must pay a licensing fee to one of these companies. This would encompass all encoding and decoding software. The current royalty rate seems to run between $1 and $25 per unit, depending on the overall number of units involved. As you might imagine, the cost of licensing the technology from these patents could financially devastate a small company that distributed freeware or shareware.

One of the reasons MP3 has gained so much popularity is the fact that it is an open standard. This doesn't mean that the technology is free; it just means that the patent holders have agreed to make the technology available to companies or individuals willing to pay a reasonable licensing fee.

NOT QUITE CD-QUALITY

While MP3 does sound good, it is still not CD-quality. When you compress an audio file down to one-tenth of its original size, something has got to give. The concept of perceptual coding in this case is to toss out the data that isn't relevant. If the human ear cannot hear above or below a certain frequency, what is the point of wasting all that disk space? When encoding a WAVE (or other standard audio) file into an MP3 file, all data you can't (or, at least, shouldn't be able to) hear is permanently deleted.

In theory, a WAVE file encoded to MP3 is one-tenth its original size and still retains all the sound quality of the original WAVE file. There are some who argue this is not so. There has been a popular notion as of late that not only do you hear music through your ears, you also feel it as it vibrates through your body. When the frequencies that you cannot hear are removed, it is thought that your body notices that these frequencies are missing, thereby diminishing the total listening experience. Whether this is true will probably be subject to debate for years to come, but it is food for thought all the same. One relatively famous musician on a music industry panel discussing this very subject was heard to ask, "Why am I spending all this money recording and mastering my CDs using the finest studios, engineers, and producers in the world if people are just going to be listening to my music as an MP3 file?"

As MP3 becomes a more prevalent means of music distribution, music may actually be mastered for optimum playback as an MP3 file. While it can be (and often is) argued that this would be similar to beating a proverbial dead horse, you must remember that music is currently mastered to CD, cassette, vinyl, mini-disk, and even for six- or eight-channel surround sound. What's the big deal about adding one more format into the mix?

THE JOURNEY

To show you how the conversion process works, we'll follow an audio file on its way to become an MP3 file.

At the beginning of this journey, we have a three-minute song. It currently resides on a standard audio CD (technically known as a "Redbook" audio CD). Before this musical performance can begin its transformation into the world of MP3, it must be moved onto a computer and converted into a WAVE file. This is done through a digital extraction process that has become known as *ripping*. For the ripping process to begin, the target audio CD is placed in the CD-ROM drive of the PC, and the ripping software is engaged to perform its extraction of the target audio file. Depending on the speed of the CPU and the software itself, this process is usually completed in a minute or two. The target audio file now resides on the computer hard drive as a stereo WAVE file. Because we have chosen to retain the CD-quality characteristics of this three-minute stereo WAVE file, it is currently taking up 30 MB of disk space.

 Note

For explicit details on how to rip and encode audio into MP3, refer to Chapters 3 and 4.

The next step in the transformation process is to encode the WAVE file into an MP3 file. During the process, some of the audio content of the WAVE file will be thrown out and the overall size of the file will be compacted down to 10 percent of its original size. In this case, the encoding process is accomplished within the computer environment with encoding software. The former 30 MB WAVE file is now a 3 MB MP3 file and is ready for playback.

The user now has two playback options: software or hardware. For simplicity sake, let's take the software route. As you know by reading this book, there are many different software players available for download as freeware and shareware. So if you have already finished Chapter 1, you have already installed either the Winamp or the Sonique software-based MP3 player into your computer (or MacAmp for Macintosh). All that's left to do is to load the MP3 file into your player and listen to the music. Once you press play, the MP3 decoder in your player (using the processor in your computer for horsepower) converts the MP3 file into something you can hear — music.

Figure 8-1 is a chronological chart that simulates the journey an audio file takes on its way to rebirth as an MP3 file.

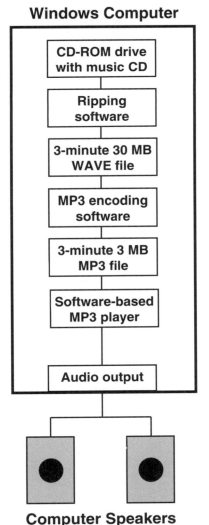

Figure 8-1

A graphic simulation of the journey an audio file takes on its way to becoming an MP3.

THE TRUTH ABOUT ENCODING

The last few paragraphs mentioned encoding and decoding a time or two. In simple terms, when you encode a standard audio file to an MP3 file, you are converting it to a different file format. How long this conversion process will take has a lot to do with the software you are using. The Xing encoder (a component of Xing's AudioCatalyst) will encode an audio file faster than any other commercially available software, while some of the freeware you might find on the Internet could easily take twenty minutes to encode one short song into a three-minute MP3 file. If you've got lots of time and no money, go for the freeware. The rest of you need to get Xinged. Remember that during the encoding process, much of the program material in the audio file is removed, resulting in a much smaller file (10 percent of the original). Regardless of what you may have heard, when you throw away 90 percent of the sound file, the overall audio quality is going to suffer. There are, however, a couple of factors that end up lessening the negative effect of removing material on the sound quality of an MP3 file.

One variable in the sound quality of an MP3 file is the encoding software. Not all encoding software is going to give you the same results. The Xing encoder, found in both Xing's AudioCatalyst and the MusicMatch Jukebox software, provides good results, while the results from some freeware and shareware applications are not quite as good. Buggy encoding software may not only tie up your computer for long periods of time, but may also mean less than optimal sound quality in your MP3 files. Do it your way; just remember there's a reason why some stuff is free.

One more determining factor is the quality of the source audio before the ripping and encoding process takes place. If it sounds great to begin with, your chances of having a decent-sounding MP3 file is multiplied greatly. In most cases, music ripped from a CD that has been recorded and mastered in a world-class facility is going to retain a lot more sparkle and presence after the conversion process than, for example, a song that was recorded and mastered under less than optimum conditions.

One exception is recordings that are mainly acoustic in nature. MP3 files in which the program material is an acoustic piano and human voice, for instance, may sound noticeably dull in comparison to the original recording. To say that MP3 rocks is more true than one would think, which brings us to the next determining element — the type of music. For some reason, music from the rock, blues, and R&B genres seems to make the transition from CD to MP3 still sounding pretty good. Loud, hard-driving music tends to lack the subtle nuances that disappear during the encoding process.

You are able to greatly enhance the listening experience of an MP3 file by using an equalizer (standard in both the Winamp and Sonique MP3 players) to boost the signal in certain frequencies. Because every recording has its own unique characteristic, and because individual tastes vary so widely, equalizer settings will vary from song to song and person to person.

DECODING

The heart of any MP3 player (software- or hardware-based) is the decoder. What the decoder does is convert the MP3 file into something you can hear — in this case, music. For each software-based MP3 player to work, the interface controls (volume, playlist, EQ, and so forth) must be built on top of a decoder of some sort. The decoder uses your computer's processor to decode the MP3 file and convert it into audio. As you may have already guessed, no two decoders work or sound exactly the same.

Within the MP3 community, the AMP decoder is without a doubt the most well-known software-based decoder. Developed by Tomislav Uzelac, the AMP decoder was the heart and soul of the original releases of both the MacAmp and Winamp MP3 players. This would change in June 1998 when Nullsoft, the makers of Winamp, changed over from AMP to their own decoder, Nitrane. In the meantime, Tomislav Uzelac became a principal of a company called PlayMedia and, in March 1999, sued Nullsoft claiming that Nitrane was a derivative of AMP and not entirely Nullsoft's creation. Whether Nullsoft actually owes royalties to PlayMedia and whether this conflict will make it to trial or be settled out of court is yet to be seen.

WHAT IS MPEG-7?

It seems that the successor to the yet-to-be-released MP4 spec would be MP5. But there are references to MPEG-7 all over the Internet. MPEG-7 is Multimedia Content Description Interface. In essence, there is so much information available on the Web in the form of video, audio, graphics, 3-D models, and more that a standardized way of describing and categorizing these items needs to be developed. MPEG-7 will extend the capabilities of today's solutions for identifying content by recognizing more data types and by standardizing a language that will define description schemes (Description Definition Language, or DDL for short). Because the nature of content delivery is evolving, the MPEG-7 specification could move beyond the Internet to include yet-to-be-implemented forms of broadcast media.

In short, MPEG-7 is being developed to make searching for and finding audio, video, and multimedia content a much easier task. Hopefully the implementation of the MPEG-7 standard in July 2001 will help everyone zero in on precisely what we're looking for on the Internet and beyond.

SAY IT AIN'T SO

There is an ugly rumor going around that MP3 has become more popular than sex. It hasn't. At least, not yet. The operators of several major Internet search engines claim that next to sex, MP3 is the most requested inquiry.

BELIEVE IT WHEN YOU HEAR IT

Is MP4 better than MP3? The real MPEG-4 still wasn't up and running when this book went to press, so it is impossible to give an accurate answer. MPEG AAC (see Chapter 7) does seem to have slightly better sound quality and a 30 percent smaller file size than MP3. Whether the new and improved versions of MPEG audio (AAC and MPEG-4) will achieve the popularity of their older and still very popular cousin MP3, is yet to be seen. Part of the reason is that MP3 is, for all practical purposes, an open standard. For $30, a consumer can buy software that will rip and encode audio into MP3. The developers holding the patents for AAC and MPEG-4 are probably not going to let their development tools be released to the general public for a price that most of us can reasonably afford. As you may have read, the record industry felt someone dropped the ball with MP3, and they don't plan on letting this happen twice. So the bottom line is that MPEG-4 will sound better than MP3, but chances are the cost and the hassle associated with using MPEG-4 may prevent a mass migration from MP3 to MPEG-4, at least in the near future.

BEFORE WE GO

No one could have predicted the popularity that MP3 has achieved since it made the jump from cult to mainstream in 1998. MP3 means different things to different people and, without a doubt, the repercussions of the entire MP3 movement is going to be felt for many years to come.

The Legalities
of MP3

9

*But take away their lawsuits and lobbying and the RIAA's power and
influence is greatly diminished. This should remind all that the battle for the
next millennium of music cannot and should not be fought in courtrooms or
back rooms. It is a battle for the consumer's heart, ears and pocketbook.*

—*Michael Robertson*

IN THIS CHAPTER

- Your Rights

- Enforcement

- Legislation

- Pirate Web Sites

- Internet Radio

- Music on Demand

From the start of the so-called MP3 revolution, there has been rumor, speculation, and a lot of inaccurate information about what an individual can or
cannot do with MP3. While this chapter isn't meant to be an all-encompassing
legal guide on the subject, it will give you the basic information about the laws
that are currently on the books. One thing you should know about law: It is subject to interpretation. We may read the text of a law and think we understand its
meaning when in reality we don't have a clue. When a dispute over the interpretation of a law arises, the dispute quite often ends up court. If the case isn't settled before trial, a judge makes a ruling; and unless someone is willing to spend
the time and money to attempt to get the ruling overturned by a higher court,
the ruling stands. This is knows as *case law*. There are currently few examples of

case law regarding MP3 specifically, but it is possible to speculate how current laws and rulings are likely to affect individual usage. Pay attention to this chapter; it will help keep you out of trouble when using MP3.

 Warning

We are not attorneys. Neither the authors nor MP3.com shall be held liable or responsible to any person or entity with respect to any loss or damages arising from the information contained in this chapter. The information provided herein is on an "as-is" basis. You have been warned! Ultimately, you are responsible for your own destiny.

YOUR RIGHTS

So what exactly are your rights in listening to and making copies of music? Before we go any further, there is something that you need to know: When you go down to your favorite retail store and buy a CD, you have purchased only a physical copy of the CD; you don't own the content (in other words, the music). It's sort of like a software license — you merely own the right to use it. There are also restrictions. For example, you have only bought the right to listen to the music privately and not in a commercial setting. Legally, you cannot make copies and distribute them to your friends and family. The record industry has accepted that the practice of making personal copies of records, CDs, and tapes is a fact of life and that it is impossible to prevent the average consumer from doing so. Initially, they were happy with extracting a 3 percent levy on blank media and 2 percent on the sale of each digital recording device (such as DAT). The explosion of MP3 changed all that, and now it is going to be next to impossible to control blank media in an online environment because it is virtual.

What are you allowed to do? If you were to rip the contents of a CD you just purchased and encode it into MP3 files for your own personal use, you would not be breaking any laws (thanks to the Home Recording Act, covered in depth later in the chapter) as long as you made only one copy for your own personal use. If you were to make copies of the MP3 files and distribute them amongst your friends or post them on the Internet, you would be breaking the law. Don't break the law.

ENFORCEMENT

So who comes after you if you break copyright law by putting up your own pirate Web site? You might be surprised. It's not the FBI, the Secret Service, or even your local sheriff. In such a case, you would get the pleasure of dealing with music industry attorneys who specialize in extracting the maximum amount of money allowed by law from you. You see, breaking copyright law is not a criminal action but a civil one, although depending on the scope of the alleged violation, it is possible that criminal charges could be filed as well. As in all areas of the law, this too is subject to interpretation.

So you might be asking yourself, "What could happen to me? I'm just one person, and why would anyone really care what I do?" Well, in this case, we are talking about the record industry, which is a $40-billion-a-year business. They do not take kindly to unauthorized distribution of their products, free or otherwise. Before the passage of the Digital Millennium Copyright Act, record companies didn't bother going after an individual if music was being distributed illegally online. Instead, they sought damages from the Internet service provider, university, or business that owned the server on which the illegally copied and distributed files resided at the time of distribution. This has now changed, and you can expect to see record companies, publishing companies, and in some cases the artists themselves going after an individual or company involved in the unauthorized distribution of their copyright-protected intellectual property (i.e., music in the form of MP3 files).

Let's take a look at the damages that can be levied against an individual or company that is illegally distributing music in the form of MP3 files (or any format, for that matter). Current U.S. copyright law allows the owner of copyrighted material to recover a minimum of $500 per violation and a maximum of $20,000 per violation. If the individual or company is found to have been selling or giving away copyright-protected music while knowing that their behavior was illegal, the amount jumps to a staggering $100,000 per violation. It could get very expensive. Steer clear of any illegal behavior. In other words, don't put someone else's music on a server for distribution.

If someone decides to make an example of you and take you to court, they could end up owning everything you have or expect to have for many years to come. If you don't like the law, then lobby to have it changed. There's been a rumor floating around for some time that the record industry may make an example of a few not-so-lucky individuals as a lesson to the rest of us. Don't let it be you.

LEGISLATION

As both consumers and content providers of music, we are affected by three important pieces of legislation that were passed in the last decade: The Home Recording Act, the Digital Performance Right in Sound Recording Act, and the Digital Millennium Copyright Act. The following sections offer a few of the highlights of these laws.

The Home Recording Act

When the Home Recording Act was passed in 1992, the great threat to the record industry was digital audio tape (DAT) recorders. It was assumed that these cassette-like digital tape players would be snapped up by the general public, and that everyone that would be making digital copies of audio CDs and selling them or giving them away. While DAT flourished overseas, court injunctions kept the format out of the hands of U.S. consumers until this law was passed. As part of this law, every consumer DAT machine sold in the U.S. is equipped with one of the serial copying management systems (or SCMS, pronounced scuzmuz). SCMS prevents the user from making a digital copy of a DAT tape. By 1992, DAT had become the de facto standard for recording studios because of its high quality of sound and relatively inexpensive tapes. This legislation also applies to all new digital recording technologies, including MP3. If a manufacturer develops a device that can record virtually identical digital copies of a CD or other music format, then it is covered by this legislation.

One of the advantages of this 1992 legislation is that it exempts consumers from being sued for copyright violation when they record music for private, noncommercial use. Another provision of the law allows the record labels and music publishers to collect a small fee on all blank media that is sold. This includes blank tapes, CDs, and any other type of media that may be developed that could be used to play music. For each digital recording device, such as a DAT recorder, sold another fee is paid to the record labels and music publishers. While songwriters and recording artists are supposed to receive a portion of these funds, that does not appear to be happening

Digital Performance Right in Sound Recording Act of 1995

Unlike the Home Recording Act, the Digital Performance Right in Sound Recording Act of 1995 does take online distribution of music into consideration. Before the passage of this law, sound recordings were the only U.S. copyrighted works denied the right of public performance. With the explosion of a number of new delivery systems for music and sound, there was a real need to protect the rights of the musicians and songwriters as well as allow them to authorize the use of their intellectual property. Currently covered under this law is delivery of content via interactive services, digital cable audio services, satellite music services, and commercial online music providers, as well as any audio technology yet to be developed and implemented. As you might imagine, delivery of music via MP3 fits into this category.

If you're not in the music business, you probably have no idea what mechanical royalties are. Aside from publishing income, the songwriter is entitled to what is known as a mechanical royalty, a payment for each physical record, CD, or tape that is manufactured and sold. The Digital Performance Right in Sound Recording Act of 1995 allows for MP3 files to be considered sound recordings, and, therefore, the songwriter is entitled to be paid a mechanical royalty for each MP3 sold.

The Digital Millennium Copyright Act

On October 28, 1998, President Bill Clinton signed into law the Digital Millennium Copyright Act of 1998 (DMCA). This law implements two global treaties whose purpose is to protect creative works in the digital era. One of the purposes of this law is to prohibit the manufacture and distribution of software and hardware designed with the express purpose of cracking the encryption codes of copyright-protected online content. One such example would be software that would allow users to crack the encryption scheme that prevents Liquid Audio's Liquid Tracks from being copied. There is supposedly software that can convert a2b music files and Liquid Audio 3.0 files into WAVE files. Developing, distributing, or using this type of software could set you up for both civil and criminal prosecution.

Another provision of this law includes important language that clarifies the rights of copyright owners and specifies the responsibilities of Internet service providers in guarding against online piracy. The DMCA also contains some critical provisions regarding the licensing of music on the Internet as well as amending the Digital Performance Right in Sound Recording Act of 1995 in a way that will bring it up to date with current advances in technology.

AND THEN CAME WIPO

The World Intellectual Property Organization (WIPO) treaties were negotiated in December 1996 by more than one hundred nations at the World Intellectual

Property Organization Diplomatic Conference in Geneva, Switzerland. The purpose of these treaties is to secure copyright protections on the Internet and strengthen copyright law on a worldwide basis. By bringing international copyright law up to date, these treaties are making it possible to fight piracy of American products in foreign countries (and vice versa). The only changes in U.S. law required by the WIPO treaties concern picking electronic locks (software cracks) in the copy protection schemes of music software as is covered by the Digital Millennium Copyright Act. In layman's terms, this means the U.S. will need to implement and enforce laws that will more severely punish those who create, distribute, and use software that defeats the copy protection schemes built into software applications and music files. Once this is done, the U.S. will be in compliance with the spirit and intent of the WIPO treaties.

PIRATE WEB SITES

Pirate Web sites are a bad thing. Why? Well, how about the musicians? Musicians get paid for their live performances, and also make a portion of their livings by selling recordings of their music. If enough people give the music away for free over the Internet, they won't be able to sell enough records to justify the expense of recording another album. If an artist chooses to make promotional copies available as a free MP3 file to fans, that is the musician's choice. If someone else chooses to make it available for free without permission, it could put an end to the musician's recording career. Few people would disagree that CDs are too expensive, but giving away copies of an artist's music is not the solution. Once sales drop below a certain number, the artist gets dropped by his or her label. In short, if you're a music fan, support your favorite musician by buying the music instead of stealing it.

In 1998, the Recording Industry Association of America (RIAA) sent thousands of educational or warning letters to music Web sites that were violating artist and record company rights. This marked a 400 percent increase over the number of letters sent out only one year earlier. The RIAA reports that the majority of these Web sites were shut down.

In January 1998, the RIAA settled lawsuits against three alleged Internet music pirates accused of violating federal copyright laws by reproducing and distributing copyrighted sound recordings without authorization. The RIAA received injunctions to stop their illegal activity, but decided against collecting monetary damages as long as the defendants never resumed their illegal activity. In May 1998, the RIAA sued two more music sites that were illegally distributing full-length songs for download. The RIAA received monetary damages from the defendants as well as permanent injunctions. The defendants were also required to perform community service. While there was no exact figure given as to the monetary damages received by the RIAA from the defendants in the lawsuits, their legal fees alone were probably staggering by the standards that most of us live by. The point is that it is wrong to steal and distribute someone else's property, including music.

INTERNET RADIO

So you want to start your own Internet radio station. It is obvious that you have impeccable musical taste and you want to share it with the world. At this point, your main concerns are most likely technical in nature, as well they should be. However, there are some legal issues that need to be addressed as well.

Let's start with how the DMCA is going to affect your broadcast expenses. Because record companies own the content that we listen to, they have always felt that they should be paid something for allowing their property to be broadcast over the airwaves. Last time around, they missed out big time, since television and radio stations don't pay the record labels anything to broadcast their music. With broadcast via the Internet, it is a different story thanks to an amendment to the DMCA that was inserted at the last minute. Once this law goes into effect, so-called Internet radio broadcasters will owe a fee to the record companies. The amount of the fee and how it will be calculated has yet to be decided.

You might be wondering why you should have to pay a fee at all. The record companies own the copyright on the performance. Because, potentially, you are sharing that performance with the entire world, they feel you owe them a piece of the action (so to speak). So what if your Internet radio station is something you do for fun and noncommercial? Too bad, you are still obligated by law to pay some sort of fee to the owners of the performance copyright. There could be a sliding fee scale. For example, if you were using a SHOUTcast server and the maximum number of people who could connect to your station was twelve, a modest fee might be charged. At this point, it is too early to know.

If you plan on being a Webcaster, your second tier of payments is going to go to ASCAP and BMI, respectively. These two performance rights organizations represent most of the songwriters and publishers in the U.S. So in addition to paying the owners of the sound recordings, you also have to pay a blanket fee to the songwriters and publishers who own the songs themselves.

ASCAP

The best place to start this search is at ASCAP's Web site (www.ascap.com). By clicking on the licensing link and following it to the relevant Web page, you can download the "ASCAP Experimental License Agreement for Internet Sites on the World Wide Web —Version 2.0" as a PDF (Adobe Acrobat) file. There are three rate schedules to choose from, but the bottom line is that you are required to pay a minimum of $250 per quarter to ASCAP for the right to play their music on your Web site.

BMI

Begin at the BMI Web site (www.bmi.com), and follow the links to the licensing Web page, where you can download the most current version of the "BMI Web Site Music Performance Agreement" as an Adobe Acrobat file. Section 4 deals with the question of a minimum fee, which comes to $500 a year. Now this doesn't mean you won't have to pay more than $500; just think of it as a deposit on what you may end up owing at the end of the year. If your radio station generates revenue, the fee goes up from there. But, if you are running a totally non-revenue-generating radio station just for the fun of it, the chances are good that you will only have to pay that $500 a year to BMI. The current BMI agreement is good through June 2000.

Total Base Cost

Without even taking into consideration the yet-to-be-decided fees that will affect Webcasters when the DMCA goes into effect, you're out $1,500 before you ever broadcast a minute of music. So what happens if you don't contact anybody and just take the attitude that you're a pirate radio station? While it's mere speculation, ASCAP, BMI, and the RIAA will probably eventually catch up with you and make you pay up — or shut you down. In a worst-case scenario, they could sue you.

An Inexpensive Option

Here's an option that some underground Webcasters are using that can bypass the RIAA, ASCAP, BMI, and just about everyone else. Are you ready? One-hundred-percent original programming. If you own the content (music) or have the written permission from the songwriter, the publisher, and the owner of the actual recording, you're a winner. The downside is that you won't be playing popular music, but the upside is that you'll be exposing new artists to the world. This is a concept that is about to take off with a few medium-sized independent record labels, and it is sure to catch on as an inexpensive way for the independent Webcaster to be heard on a worldwide basis.

MUSIC ON DEMAND

Like MP3 and the explosion of music available on the Internet, the concept of music on demand or interactive music programming has created some controversy. The record labels had worried (and with good reason) that if an individual could go to a Web site and program music into an online radio station (or jukebox), they would quit buying music and just listen to music via the Web.

Imagine Radio (www.imagineradio.com) is probably the most visible example of a pioneer in this area, allowing users to create their own custom online radio station. With Imagine Radio, it is possible to choose a genre (rock, for instance) and then set the preferences so only music from the artists you like will play on your custom radio station. The user can also choose whether to make this choice of music available to others who venture into the online world of Imagine Radio. If you think an artist or song stinks, you simply tweak the preferences on your station and you never have to hear that artist again. Empowerment, to say the least. What if you were able to program your station so that all you ever heard was Motley Crue? This "all Crue all the time" concept is why the record industry had an amendment added to the Digital Millennium Copyright Act to prevent it from ever coming to pass.

Here's the deal: In a three-hour period, the same song can be played only three times (regardless of who the recording artist is) and the same recording artist can only be played three times as well. Three and three, then you're done until the next three-hour time frame. Remember that this restriction applies only to music on demand situations and has nothing to do with Web radio broadcasts. It is likely that this restriction would not apply to an Internet radio broadcast or an Internet simulcast from an AM or FM radio station. However, here's a situation that could be considered a gray area: What if an Internet radio station took requests? Would this law apply in that situation? We'll just have to wait and see.

So how do you get around a law like this? By owning the content, of course. If Sony Records were to build an online interactive subscription service that featured content from only Sony artists, this particular law would not apply. They own the content, after all, and can do what they want with it. In the future, you can expect to see record labels creating their own interactive subscription-based areas on their Web sites in which users can (for a monthly fee) listen to their favorite artists over and over again. Chances are that interactive music programming may be the e-commerce future of MP3.

OPM

Using other people's music is a controversial subject at best. Many of you feel music should be free. Everyone has to earn a living, and musicians are no different. But some people still don't get it. So here's a semi-fictitious scenario. Just remember that it could happen.

You're a cool, fifteen-year-old computer genius with a cable modem connection and a Pentium III computer. Every afternoon before your parents get home from work, you turn your computer system into an FTP site and make the more than one thousand MP3 files in your personal collection available to anyone who shows up. In the last month alone, more than ten thousand MP3 files have been downloaded off of your system. As fate would have it, Big Booty Records, the home of your favorite recording artists, has shown a drop in sales of 35 percent in the last six months. This drastic reduction in revenue can be directly attributed to the fact that the target audience of Big Booty's recording artists is under twenty-one, computer literate, and has jumped on the free MP3 bandwagon with a vengeance. The decision to lay off fifty of their trusted employees and drop half of the recording artists from their roster doesn't weigh lightly on these independent record executives, but they have no choice; sales are flat and getting flatter by the minute. You, in fact, have changed the world. You've put people who were pursuing their dream of working in the music business out of work.

Because this is fiction, let's take it a little farther. The owners of Big Booty Records and their lawyers decide to make an example of someone. Their purpose is to recover lost revenue and to use this example to stop piracy of their product. Unbeknownst to you, the babe you met in an MP3 chatroom on AOL is really a dude named Fred who works for Big Booty Records. Fred is looking for individuals who are stealing his company's music and giving it away in the form of MP3 files. In an effort to impress, you send an e-mail to Fred, bragging about the fact you were able to facilitate the download of one thousand MP3 files from your home computer in one month. Using this information and doing a little detective work, the lawyers at Big Booty find out who you are and where you live. One night during dinner, there is a knock at the door, and guess what? You're busted! Your computer is confiscated, your parents are served with a lawsuit for $10 million, and life as you know it is over. It's going to cost more money than your family has to fight the lawsuit. Big Booty is making an example out of you to show the world what happens to anyone caught stealing their music. U.S. copyright law allows a minimum of $500 per violation, and you're claiming ten thousand downloads in one month. Do the math. Because you are a minor and the computer belongs to your parents, they are being held liable for your actions.

Okay, this is a worst-case scenario, but it is possible. You might think because you're under eighteen or have no assets, nothing is going to happen to you. Don't count on it. Right now, the loss of revenue to MP3 pirates is very small in comparison to what it will be. There are already massive layoffs in the record industry, and some record labels are going out of business forever. At some point, MP3 pirates may be blamed for the downturn in sales, and when this happens the record labels are going to start looking for someone to prosecute. Don't let it be you.

IN SEARCH OF MP3

When you are interested in finding something on the Web, there is no better place to start than with one of the many available search engines. Lycos was the first major portal to jump on the MP3 bandwagon with a dedicated MP3 search engine (mp3.lycos.com). While the Lycos MP3 search engine is a great resource for MP3 fans, it is also a great source of distress for the worldwide record industry. It seems that, when searching for free MP3 files on the Web with the Lycos search engine, the results turn up more content from so-called pirate Web sites than from legitimate sources. The RIAA is considering filing a lawsuit against Lycos to get them to shut down their dedicated MP3 search engine.

Whether Lycos, Yahoo, and any of the other search engines are breaking the law by providing links to pirate Web sites containing MP3 files has yet to be decided in a court of law. We will just have to wait and see, but when you think about it, that's the whole story with MP3, isn't it? Wait and see what happens next.

ONE LAST THOUGHT

We hope that this chapter has given you a good overview of what the legal issues are regarding MP3 and the Internet. Remember that while this chapter is meant to be informative, it is not a comprehensive legal guide to music and MP3 on the Internet; for that, you need a lawyer. While there are laws on the books that are meant to protect and regulate the delivery and distribution of content on the Internet, it is still pretty crazy out there, and it will probably get crazier as time goes on. Don't forget that ignorance of the law doesn't protect you if someone decides they are going to sue you for broadcasting or distributing their music over the Internet without their permission. Just use a little common sense, and stay tuned to MP3.com, the most comprehensive MP3 resource on the Internet!

Glossary

ASCAP   The acronym for the American Society of Composers, Authors, and Publishers. ASCAP is a performing rights licensing organization dedicated to protecting the intellectual property rights of its members.

BMI   The acronym for Broadcast Music Inc., a nonprofit performing rights organization.

Burning a CD   When archiving data to a write-once CD, you are permanently burning the data onto the CD. Therefore, CD drives that are used to write data to blank CDs have picked up the name "CD burners," and the act of transferring data to blank CDs is known as "burning a CD."

CODEC   A synonym for a technology that handles the encode and decode functions of an audio file.

DAT   The acronym for digital audio tape, a format for storing music on magnetic tape.

EQ   The abbreviation for equalizer or graphic equalizer, which is an electronic mechanism for adjusting the volume of selected frequency ranges.

Decoder	For the purposes of this book, a decoder is what converts an MP3 file into something that you can hear.
Encoder	In the case of audio, an encoder converts an audio file into another format. MP3 encoding software is how you would convert a WAVE file into an MP3 file.
GMC	The acronym for the Genuine Music Coalition. This coalition was created by Liquid Audio to add legitimacy to the MP3 movement. Coalition members display the Genuine Music mark on their Web sites, and all MP3 content distributed by coalition members is encoded with the coalition's digital watermark technology (for identification purposes).
ID3 Tag	The ID3 Tag is inserted at the end of an MP3 file and can contain artist, title, and album information
ISP	The acronym for Internet Service Provider, a company that provides access to the Internet.
kbps (or kps)	This is an abbreviation for kilobytes per second, which is a rate at which data transfers. Different applications list it as *kbps* or *kps*. They mean the same thing.
MPEG	The acronym for the Moving Picture Experts Group, an organization that selects standards for digital audio and video compression. "MPEG" is also used to refer to the standard itself.
MP3	MPEG Level 1 Layer 3. Layer 3 is the audio layer of MPEG-1.
Normalize	The normalize process is intended to boost the signal of an audio file to its maximum level without causing distortion.
Playlist	The playlist is a series of songs (or audio files). In MP3 players such as Winamp, MP3 files can be entered into a playlist and set to play in a specific order.
Preamp	Short for preamplifier, which boosts weak audio signals before they are fed into the amplifier.

Ripping   A slang term for digital audio extraction. If you were ripping a track from an audio CD, you would in essence be performing a digital extraction.

SDMI   The acronym for the Secure Digital Music Initiative (see Chapter 7 for details).

Skins   With regards to software-based MP3 players (Winamp is the classic example), skins are a visual cover that literally fits over the top of the player. You can change the look of your MP3 player while still retaining all the functionality of the standard version. A variety of free skins are available for download at both the Winamp (`http://www.winamp.com`) and MacAmp (`http://www.macamp.com`) Web sites.

Streaming   Streaming audio actually begins playback before the entire file has been downloaded. By the default and the sheer size of the installed base, RealNetworks RealAudio is considered the classic example of streaming audio.

Tagging   Adding information to the ID3 Tag of an MP3 file.

Appendix: MP3.com Artist Agreement

MP3.COM MUSIC SUBMISSION AGREEMENT

This agreement describes the legal relationship between you (an individual artist, or, in the case where you are involved with a band, an individual acting as the legal representative of your band) and Zco, Inc. (a corporation doing business as MP3.com, and referred to in this agreement as "we" or "us"). Please read it very carefully. **By clicking on the "I AGREE" button below, you indicate that you agree to be bound by all of the terms and conditions of this agreement. Further, by submitting any music or other content to us, you indicate that you agree to be bound by this agreement.**

This agreement addresses two different types of situations. The first situation is our "Standard Program," where you supply songs and/or other content to us and allow us to include your material in our database which we make freely available over the Web, and allow us to make certain other uses of your material. The second situation is our Digital Automatic Music ["DAM"] System, under which you supply us with at least one song which we make can make freely available, and a number of other songs which we can distribute on your behalf on compact disk. The legal terms which apply to the Standard Program are described below in Part I. The legal terms which apply to the DAM System are described in Part II. One or the other of these parts may not apply to you. Legal terms applicable to both situations, **including your right to terminate this agreement and all licenses granted to us at any time**, are described in Part III.

Part I: Standard Program

If you provide us with sound recordings, musical works and/or other material (such as pictures, videos, song lyrics, etc.) for use as part of our Standard Program (collectively "Standard Program Material"), the following terms apply:

1. Standard Program License Grant. You hereby grant to us, and by the act of delivering Standard Program Material to us grant to us, a nonexclusive, worldwide, royalty-free license to: (a) reproduce, distribute, publicly perform, publicly display and digitally perform the Standard Program Material in whole or in part (including the right to create compilations which include your songs); (b) create and use samples of the Standard Program Material solely for the purpose of demonstrating or promoting our or your products or services; (c) use any trademarks, service marks or trade names incorporated in the Standard Program Material in connection with your material; and (d) use the name and likeness of any individuals represented in the Standard Program Material only in connection with your material.

Part II: DAM System

If you provide us with sound recordings, musical works and/or material (such as pictures, videos, song lyrics, etc.) for use as part of our DAM System, the following terms apply:

1. License Grant for Sample Song(s) and Collateral Material. As part of your participation in the DAM System you will deliver one or more songs to us which we can make widely available as samples of your work ["Sample Songs."] You may also deliver other material related to you or any of your songs ["Collateral Material"]. You hereby grant to us, and by the act of delivering Sample Songs and Collateral Material to us grant to us, a nonexclusive, worldwide, royalty-free license to: (a) reproduce, distribute, publicly perform, publicly display and digitally perform the Sample Songs and the Collateral Material in whole or in part (including the right to create compilations which include the Sample Songs and related Collateral Material); (b) create and use samples of the Sample Songs and Collateral Material solely for the purpose of demonstrating or promoting our or your products or services; (c) convert your songs from MP3 format to redbook format in order to distribute them on a DAM CD; (d) use any trademarks, service marks or trade names incorporated in the Sample Songs and/or the Collateral Material only in connection with your material; and (e) use the name and likeness of any individuals represented in the Sample Songs and/or the Collateral Material only in connection with your material.

2. License Grant for DAM Songs. As part of your participation in the DAM System you will deliver several songs to us which we can only make available on CDs as part of the DAM System ["DAM Songs"]. You hereby grant to us, and by the act of delivering DAM Songs to us grant to us, a nonexclusive, worldwide license to: (a) reproduce and distribute each DAM Song only in connection with distributing CDs containing your songs as part of our DAM System; (b) convert your songs from MP3 format to redbook format in order to distribute them on a DAM CD; and (c) use any trademarks, service marks or trade names incorporated in the DAM Songs only in connection with your material.

3. Payments. You will set the price of the CDs which contain your DAM Songs. We will pay you 50% of the Net Revenue we receive from sales of such CDs. "Net Revenue" means the gross revenues we actually receive from such sales, less only sales, use, value added, or similar taxes, customs duties, import or export taxes or levies, shipping or freight, and all returns. We will determine the amount owed to you on a quarterly basis. Within 60 days of the close of each quarter in which we have sold any CDs containing your DAM Songs, we will send you a detailed accounting statement and a check payable in U.S. Dollars in the appropriate amount, except if the amount we owe you is less than $50.00 then we will hold the money until either (i) the total cumulative amount we owe you at the end of any particular quarter is greater than $50.00, or (ii) this agreement terminates. We agree to keep accurate books and records covering all transactions related to this agreement. During the one year period following your receipt of an accounting statement you may, at your expense and upon reasonable notice, inspect our records related to that statement at our offices or at a location specified by us, provided that your inspection must not unreasonably interfere with our business. If your inspection reveals that we have underpaid you we will promptly correct the deficiency, plus 10% interest.

Part III: General Terms

The following terms apply to both the Standard Program and to the DAM System:

1. Ownership. You retain ownership of the copyrights and all other rights in your songs, subject to the non-exclusive rights granted to us under this agreement. You are free to grant similar rights to others during and after the term of this agreement.

2. Termination. You may terminate this agreement at any time by so notifying us; the agreement will terminate upon our actual receipt of such notice. We may terminate this agreement at any time by so notifying you; the agreement will terminate upon your actual receipt of such notice or three days after we have sent a notice of termination to the e-mail address which you supply to us below. Upon termination, all of our license rights terminate, except that we retain those rights necessary for us to sell any CDs or other tangible goods which we have produced prior to the date of termination which incorporate any of your Material (as defined in section 3 below). Our obligation to pay you amounts due to you under this agreement survives termination. Also, sections 3 and 6 below survive termination.

3. Representations and Warranties. The term "Material" means all material that you submit to us, including Standard Program Material, Sample Songs, DAM Songs and Collateral Material, as applicable. You represent and warrant that (a) the Material is your or your band's own original work, and contains no sampled material, (b) you have full right and power to enter into and perform this agreement, and have secured all third party consents necessary to enter into this agreement, (c) the Material does not and will not infringe on any third party's copyright, patent, trademark, trade secret or other proprietary rights, rights of publicity or privacy, or moral rights, (d) the Material does not and will not violate any law, statute, ordinance or regulation, (e) the Material is not and will not be defamatory, trade libelous, pornographic or obscene, (f) the Material does not and will not contain any viruses or other programming routines that detrimentally interfere with computer systems or data, (g) all factual assertions that you have made and will make to us are true and complete. You agree to indemnify and hold us and our customers harmless from any and all damages and costs, including reasonable attorney's fees, arising out of or related to your breach of the representations and warranties described in this section. You agree to execute and deliver documents to us, upon our reasonable request, that evidence or effectuate our rights under this agreement.

4. Determining Type of Content. We will implement and maintain business practices which enable us to accurately categorize content that you deliver to us. If we make an error in good faith, however (for example, if we erroneously categorize a song that you send to us as a "Sample Song" when in fact you intended it to be a "DAM Song") and consequently exceed our license rights, your sole and exclusive remedy will be for us to take all reasonable steps to promptly correct the error as soon as we become aware of the error.

5. Disclaimer. We provide our products and services related to this agreement "AS IS" without warranty of any kind.

6. Waiver of Certain Damages. EXCEPT FOR A BREACH OF SECTION 3 OF PART III, NEITHER YOU OR US WILL BE LIABLE FOR ANY CONSEQUENTIAL, INDIRECT, EXEMPLARY, SPECIAL OR INCIDENTAL DAMAGES ARISING FROM OR RELATING TO THIS AGREEMENT.

7. Miscellaneous. This agreement will be governed by California law, excluding conflict of law principles. Any action or proceeding arising out of or related to this agreement must be brought in a state or Federal court located in San Diego County, California, and we both irrevocably submit to the exclusive jurisdiction of such courts. All notices, requests and other communications under this agreement must be in writing (e-mail messages shall be deemed writings). This agreement sets forth the entire understanding and agreement of the parties as to this agreement's subject matter and supersedes all prior proposals, discussions or agreements with respect to such subject matter. It may be changed only by a writing signed by both parties (e-mail headers and/or plaintext signatures on e-mail messages shall be deemed signatures).

The address and phone info below will not be given out to anyone. It's only for our internal records.

Index